Wills

FOURTH EDITION

DAVID A CHATTERTON
LLB (HONS), MPHIL
SOLICITOR, TEP

SERIES EDITOR
CM BRAND, SOLICITOR

Cavendish
Publishing

Fourth edition published in Great Britain 2001 by Cavendish Publishing Limited, The Glass House, Wharton Street, London WC1X 9PX, United Kingdom
Telephone: + 44 (0)20 7278 8000 Facsimile: +44 (0)20 7278 8080
Email: info@cavendishpublishing.com
Website: www.cavendishpublishing.com

British Library Cataloguing in Publication Data

Chatterton, David A
Wills – 4th ed – (Practice notes series)
1 Wills – England 2 Wills – Wales
I Title
346.4'2'054

ISBN 1 85941 663 2

Printed and bound in Great Britain

Acknowledgments

In this fourth edition of this work, which is totally updated to include the Trustee Act 2000, I would like to acknowledge the assistance and patience of a number of people.

First, I would like to acknowledge the help and support of my wife Sheila and my son Stephen who had the monstrous task of deciphering my handwriting. I would also like to acknowledge the assistance of Cavendish Publishing for their support and encouragement.

The law is stated as at the 1st February 2001.

David A Chatterton
February 2001

Publisher's Note

For the sake of simplicity of style, 'he', 'his', etc, have been used throughout the text. 'She', 'her', etc, should be read as an alternative, where appropriate.

Contents

1 Basic Information

1.1 Introduction

This introductory chapter is intended to explain why a will is necessary and the reasons why you should advise a client to make a professionally prepared will rather than leave the devolution of his estate on death to the law of intestacy – the legal rules which the law imputes as being the intentions of a dead person where he has failed to make a will – setting out and clarifying his wishes as to the disposition of his property when he dies. It is important that the reasons and justification for a will are clearly and precisely explained to the client so that he appreciates fully the need for a will and does not begrudge the legal fees payable for preparing, drafting and executing a formal will. Above all, careful explanation must be given in layman's terms of the financial benefits which may accrue to the beneficiaries under the will from a professionally drawn up document, for example, by tax planning and the mitigation of Inheritance Tax (see Chapter 4, 'Advising the Client') and the savings that may arise on death when the will has to be proved.

1.2 Giving effect to the testator's wishes

(a) Advise the client that in his will he may clearly and precisely state how he wishes all his property (whether it be his house, car, bank accounts or stocks/shares) to pass on death and arrange, so far as the law will permit, for his relatives to receive his assets on his death, subject to the administration of his estate by his appointed personal representatives.

(b) Point out to the client that by the terms of his will he may nominate a person or persons (an executor/executors) to carry out his wishes and arrange for the distribution of his estate to his next of kin, friends and favourite charities according to the wishes he has laid down in his will.

(c) Advise the client that if he does not appoint an executor, an administrator will be nominated by law (by r 22(1) of the Non-Contentious Probate Rules 1987 SI 1987/2024) to carry out the distribution of the estate. If, however, the client appoints an executor, he will be the first person entitled to prove the will and administer the client's estate (see r 20 of the Non-Contentious Probate Rules 1987).

By nominating an executor in his will, the client may appoint a person he trusts to carry out the distribution of his estate and, where appropriate, he should be advised to appoint businesslike or professional people (for example, solicitors or accountants) as executors because they will have the expertise to maximise the possible financial and fiscal advantages on the distribution of the estate. (As to the choice of executors and trustees, see Chapter 4, 'Advising the Client'.)

• Advise the client that by the terms of his will he may express his wishes as to disposal of his body on his death and the possible use of parts of his body for transplant surgery.

The following should be noted:

(a) it has been suggested by some legal writers that it is preferable to leave directions in a separate letter addressed to a close relative, as, sometimes, the will is not opened or even discovered until after the funeral. If this is done, the solicitor should retain a copy of the letter with the completed draft will;

(b) it is possible, by writing to the DSS, Alexander Fleming House, Elephant and Castle, London SE1 6BY, to obtain a memorandum as to gifts of bodies for anatomical examination. By s 4 of the Anatomy Act 1984, a written request by a dead person is binding on the executors unless any relative objects;

(c) as to the use of the body for therapeutic purposes, reference should be made to the Human Tissue Act 1961 – this Act is, *inter alia*, the authority for removal of the eyes;

(d) the executors and deceased's family are not legally bound by the deceased's funeral and burial wishes, other than the requirement that they must give effect to a direction against cremation which is effective in law.

1.3 Preventing intestacy and possible family provision claims

(a) Make it clear to the client that if he does not make a will, his estate will devolve or pass according to the law of intestacy, which could mean that the persons who become entitled to the bulk of his estate may not be those whom he would wish to benefit on his death (for the rules as to the devolution of an estate on intestacy, refer to Chapter 2, 'The Relevant Law').

(b) Advise the client about the possible rights of claimants under the Inheritance (Provision for Family and Dependants) Act 1975 which gives rights to, *inter alia*, mistresses and divorced spouses (who have not remarried) to make a claim on a person's estate on his death.

(c) Advise the client who fears a possible family provision claim under the above Act as to s 21, which enables a statement to be made, either oral or written, as to the reasons why the testator does not wish to make provision for a particular person. The statement may be embodied in the will or a contemporaneous written and signed statement may be placed with the will giving reasons why no provision is made for any person. Such a statement is admissible as evidence of the facts stated therein.

1.4   Special clauses

(a) Advise the client that provision may be made in a will for special purposes, for example, guardianship of minor children, or provisions permitting the deceased's personal representatives to carry on the business if, for example, he was a sole trader (see Chapter 5, 'Precedent Clauses'). Clauses are often inserted appointing guardians of minors on the death of a parent – a guardian may act jointly with a surviving parent (s 3 of the Guardianship of Minors Act 1971).

(b) In order to provide for the financial support and maintenance of minor children, the client's instructions should be taken as to whether he wishes to insert in the will a clause extending or varying the powers of maintenance and advancement of capital (incorporated in ss 31 and 32 of the Trustee Act 1925) and he should be fully advised as to the effect of such clauses. These are usually fairly standard in professionally prepared wills; see Chapter 5 for a standard clause to be inserted in such circumstances.

(c) Advise the client as to the insertion of other special clauses, for example, extension of investment powers of trustees under the Trustee Investment Act 1961, or exclusion of certain costly income/interest apportionment rules, for example, *Howe v Earl of Dartmouth* (1802) 7 Ves 137 (for standard clauses to provide for these circumstances, see, also, Chapter 5).

1.5   Tax and estate planning

(a) Emphasise the tax-saving advantages which may accrue to the estate by careful use of a will as an estate planning instrument. It should be clearly explained to the client that a professionally drafted will can effect substantial Inheritance Tax savings for a deceased person's relatives, so that they will receive an increased share of his estate and not be compelled to pay the potential full charge to tax (see Chapter 4).

(b) Advise the client that he may make lifetime gifts to his relatives and, if he survives them for a period of seven years from the date of the gift, no tax will be payable (see s 3A of the Inheritance Tax Act 1984, as added by the Finance Act 1986).

(c) Advise the client of the annual £3,000 exemption, small gift exemption, etc (see, generally, Inheritance Tax Act 1984 and 4.3) and such devices as equalisation of estates between spouses and the discretionary trust which can be used to mitigate Inheritance Tax liability.

1.6   Administrative expense-saving

The absence of a will effectively creates a vacuum and, therefore, when a person dies without making a will, substantial expense may be incurred in tracing whether a will has actually been made (see Chapter 8, 'Answers to Common Questions', where advice is given on how to ensure that any will made by the deceased is easily found). Extra expense may also be incurred in tracing relatives where no will is found.

Generally, it is easier and less costly to have a will than to be involved in proving and administering an estate where no will has been made. Not only is it, in fact, more costly to obtain a grant of letters of administration to an estate than a grant of probate in respect of a deceased's will, but also, the trusts which may well arise under the intestacy rules as at present can be very costly in terms of administration expenses and, in practical terms, are unlikely to reflect the client's true wishes regarding the devolution of his estate.

1.7   Role of the Probate Registrar

Applications for non-contentious grants of probate or letters of administration are made to the Principal Probate Registry, the District Probate Registry or Sub-District Registry (see Chapter 9 for the addresses of these registries). 'Non-contentious business' consists of probate and administration applications which do not lead to any form of litigation and are therefore non-contentious.

Each registry has a registrar who checks that all the papers leading to a grant are in order and that the will, if any, is valid and complies with the necessary legal rules as to formalities (see Chapter 2, 'The Relevant Law' for a discussion of the general principles of law applicable).

The registrar also applies the rules which regulate non-contentious business, that is, the Non-Contentious Probate Rules 1987 SI 1987/2024, which consolidated the Non-Contentious Probate Rules 1954 and came into force on 1 January 1988.

If solicitors are in doubt as to the drafting of probate/administration papers, the registrar will usually settle them for a small fee.

1.8   Relevant legislation

The main Acts concerned with the validity of wills are:

(a) Wills Act 1837;

(b) Wills (Soldiers and Sailors) Act 1918;

(c) Pt IV, ss 17–52 of the Administration of Justice Act 1982 (which amends the previous legislation).

The powers of executors, administrators and trustees are largely derived from:

(a) Administration of Estates Act 1925;

(b) Trustee Act 1925;

(c) Law of Property Act 1925;

(d) Trustee Investment Act 1961;

(e) Trusts of Land and Appointment of Trustees Act 1996;

(f) Trustee Delegation Act 1999;

(g) Trustee Act 2000 (see, for more details, Chapter 7).

The law on intestacy can be found in the Administration of Estates Act 1925 and the Intestates' Estates Act 1952.

Family provision claims are dealt with under the Inheritance (Provision for Family) Act 1975. The Law Reform (Succession) Act 1995 has made the significant amendments referred to in the text.

The legislation on Inheritance Tax is chiefly to be found in the Inheritance Tax Act 1984 as amended by the Finance Acts, in particular, the Finance Act 1986.

For the rules of the Probate Registry, reference should be made to the Non-Contentious Probate Rules 1987 SI 1987/2024.

1.9 Living wills

Occasionally, ill and incapacitated people may be kept alive for long periods by medical treatment which, if they remained competent to decide, they might refuse, thereby facilitating death from natural causes.

Individuals can anticipate this situation by expressing wishes in advance (by 'advance directives' known as 'living wills') or delegating the right to make the decisions to someone else on their behalf.

There are, however, at present, no procedures whereby a person can delegate to another the power to consent to or refuse medical treatment.

'Living wills' (which are quite distinct from the wills discussed throughout this book), as they do not dispose of property, are means by which a person can request that certain treatment should, or should not, be given in certain circumstances if the individual is not himself competent to consent to or refuse medical treatment. There is no presumption of consent.

Recent cases, such as *Airedale NHS Trust v Bland* [1993] 2 WLR 316, HL, suggest that such advance directives may have legal effect.

Precedents of 'living wills' are available, *inter alia*, from the Voluntary Euthanasia Society (13 Princess of Wales Terrace, London W8 5PG) and the Terrence Higgins Trust (52–54 Grays Inn Road, London WC1X 8JW). Precedents of the suggested 'living wills' of both organisations are reproduced with their consent in Chapter 6 (6.6 and 6.7) and their telephone numbers are included in Chapter 9 ('Useful Addresses').

The Scottish decision of *Law Hospital Trust v Johnstone* (1996) by Lord Cameron of Lochbroon is an interesting one in which an order was made discontinuing treatment of a patient who had been in a persistent vegetative condition for some four years. The case, being Scottish, is only of persuasive authority in English law, but may have far reaching implications.

2 The Relevant Law

2.1 Introduction

The intention of this book is to emphasise the more significant points of the law relating to the subject rather than to give an exhaustive discussion of the law relating to the making and revocation of wills, intestacy and family provision.

There are a great many learned works on the law of succession ranging from such tomes as Theobald and Clark, *The Law of Wills*, Sweet & Maxwell, and *Jarman on Wills*, Sweet & Maxwell, through to the standard student text books such as Parry and Clark, *The Law of Succession*, Sweet & Maxwell. For a more thorough treatment of the subject, the reader is respectfully referred to these and other works as listed in Chapter 10, 'Further Reading'.

2.2 Definition and nature of a will

A will has been defined as 'the expression by a person of wishes which he intends to take effect only at his death' (Parry and Clark, *The Law of Succession*, p 1).

To make a valid will, a person must incorporate in a legally valid document his intentions as to the disposition of his property on death.

A will is ambulatory, that is, it does not take effect until the testator actually dies. In addition, it is effective to dispose of not only the property the testator owns at the date he makes the will, but also all property which he acquires at any time between the date of his will and his actual death (s 24 of the Wills Act 1837).

A will must be revocable at any time prior to the testator's death.

A will can effectively dispose of all the testator's property of any kind whether real or personal, vested, contingent or in remainder.

In the decision in *Re Berger* [1989] 2 WLR 147, the Court of Appeal held:

(a) that a will must contain revocable ambulatory dispositions of the deceased's property which are to be effective on death, and the testator should intend this to be so; and

(b) that it was possible to make a valid will, whatever its form or appearance or mode of expression, and irrespective of the language used, so long as it was duly executed and there was an intention to make a will. Where the document was duly executed and the document had the necessary dispositive effect and it was duly executed in accordance with English law, the intention to make a will would be presumed – this was a case in which a will written in Hebrew was held to be valid.

2.3   Capacity to make a will

Capacity to make a will depends on the testator being over 18 years of age (s 3(1A) of the Family Law Reform Act 1969) and of sound mind, memory and understanding at the time he executes the will (*Banks v Goodfellow* (1870) LR 5 QB 549).

Privileged wills (that is, wills made by soldiers in actual military service, airmen, mariners or seamen at sea) may be made by those under 18 (s 1 of the Wills (Soldiers and Sailors) Act 1918, as amended by s 3(1B) of the Family Law Reform Act 1969). It is not intended to discuss here the law relating to the capacity of those who are entitled to make privileged wills – please refer to such works as Parry and Clark, *The Law of Succession*, if you feel the testator may be entitled to privileged status and particularly be aware of the position of soldiers in Northern Ireland (*Re Jones* [1981] Fam 7) and in West Germany (*Re Colman* [1958] 1 WLR 457).

A testator, to be of sound mind, memory and understanding, must understand three matters:

(a) the effect of his wishes being carried out at his death;

(b) the extent of the property of which he is disposing; and

(c) the nature of claims on him (*Banks v Goodfellow* (1870) LR 5 QB 567).

If the testator is not of sound mind, memory and understanding at the time the will is executed, it is an invalid will. There have been a number of recent decisions on capacity emphasising the significance of establishing the mental capacity of the testator, for example, *Wilkes v Wilkes* [2000] unreported, 8 June, which confirmed that the burden of proving capacity to make a will lies with the person who seeks to uphold the will (see, also, *Worby v Rosser* [1999] 2 ITELR 59).

There is no presumption of undue influence in the law of wills, and if a party seeks to impute undue influence, he must prove it to the satisfaction of the court on the balance of probabilities (*Parfitt v Lawless* (1872) LR 2 P & D 462) – but also note the case of *Simpson v Simpson* (1989) 19 Fam LR 20, where Mowitt J held at first instance that, although the relationship existing between spouses did not itself give rise to a · presumption of undue influence, it was possible in certain circumstances that such a presumption might arise. This is a somewhat surprising decision in regard to the principles laid down in *Parfitt v Lawless*.

A blind or illiterate testator must satisfy the registrar that he understood and approved the contents at the date of execution of the will (r 13 of the Non-Contentious Probate Rules 1987 SI 1987/2024), for example, by adducing evidence that the will was read over to the testator and that he understood fully the contents of the will.

If there are suspicious circumstances, it must be proved that the testator knew and approved of the contents of the will (*Wintle v Nye* [1959] 1 WLR 284), but if the will is drawn up by a solicitor who takes any benefits under the will, this can raise a very serious disciplinary matter for the solicitor.

In *Re A Solicitor* (1975) *The Times*, 23 November, the Court of Appeal determined that a solicitor who takes a benefit under a will prepared by him is under a duty to refer the client to another solicitor who must give the client independent advice and make absolutely certain that the testator realises exactly what he is doing, otherwise the benefiting solicitor is guilty of professional misconduct and is liable to be struck off the roll of solicitors. The importance of this case is obvious to all articled clerks or newly admitted solicitors.

Re Simpson (1977) 121 Sol Jo 224 lays down a golden rule that, in the case of an aged testator or one who has suffered a serious illness, an experienced medical practitioner must be present to examine the testator's state of mind at the time he executes the will and, if he is satisfied, be an attesting witness. This is a matter for very careful consideration and depends upon your knowledge of the client, but, according to Templeman J, the rule must be applied however tactless it may seem to be. See, also, Chapter 3, 'Taking the Client's Instructions'.

2.4   Requirements of a valid will

Section 9 of the Wills Act 1837 (as amended by s 17 of the Administration of Justice Act 1982) states that:

No will shall be valid unless –

(a) it is in writing, and signed by the testator, or by some other person in his presence and by his direction; and

(b) it appears that the testator intended by his signature to give effect to the will; and

(c) the signature is made or acknowledged by the testator in the presence of two or more witnesses present at the same time; and

(d) each witness either –

(i) attests and signs the will; or

(ii) acknowledges his signature in the presence of the testator (but not necessarily in the presence of any other witness),

but no form of attestation shall be necessary.

Section 9 (as amended) is extremely important, for the most trivial breach of the provisions of the section may result in the will being held invalid, and this could well make the solicitor preparing the will liable in professional negligence. It is, therefore, advisable to include a standard form of attestation clause in every will prepared – see suggested clause at 5.26.

All wills must be in writing (except privileged wills), although the law does allow a great deal of latitude in this respect – a will may be handwritten, typed or printed.

Wills may be written on any material. Normally, of course, paper is used, but wills are acceptable on materials other than paper, for example, written on an empty egg shell (*Hodson v Barnes* (1926) 43 TLR 71). Generally, of course, wills are 'engrossed' on good quality lasting paper.

The signature must be that of the testator himself, or alternatively, he may direct another person to sign the will on his behalf, in his presence.

The testator must do all he intended to do in signing (contrast *Re Chalcraft* [1948] P 222 with other cases such as *Re Colling* [1972] 3 All ER 729) in the presence of the witnesses.

Section 9 was amended by s 17 of the Administration of Justice Act 1982, so that the testator's signature need only be intended to give effect to the will and need not, as previously, be at the foot or end of the will.

For all practical purposes, however, the testator's signature must be at the foot or end of the will, otherwise special evidence as to the contents of the will may be required on applying for a grant of probate – see 5.26 (for example, an affidavit of due execution).

The signature of the testator must be made or acknowledged in the presence of two witnesses present at the same time. This requirement is one of substantive law and must be complied with. The witnesses must actually sign their names, not print them, otherwise the Probate Registry may require an affidavit of due execution as to why they printed their names rather than signing them in the normal fashion.

The law as to the formalities for making a valid will are very explicit and must be carefully followed. If in any doubt whatsoever, use common, standard forms of attestation clause and make sure the client does everything in accordance with s 9. A beneficiary or spouse of a beneficiary who witnesses a will, loses all benefit thereunder (s 15 of the Wills Act 1837), although that person will still be a valid witness. Note, especially, the decision in *Ross v Caunters* [1980] Ch 297, where a solicitor was held professionally negligent for not pointing out that a beneficiary or spouse of a beneficiary who witnesses a will loses all benefit under that will. In the now famous case of *Esterhuizen v Allied Dunbar plc* [1998] 2 FLR 668, it was held that it was the duty of the solicitor preparing the will to take stringent care that the will was duly executed in accordance with s 9. It is now established that a solicitor must not normally send the will to the testator's home for execution.

Solicitors, for their own protection, should make an offer in writing in the following terms: (a) that the client may visit the solicitor's office to execute the will there; (b) if the client prefers, the solicitor or a member of his staff may visit the client's home to assist him in the correct execution of the will; (c) if the client prefers, he may make his own arrangements.

The solicitor would be prudent to confirm the testator's instructions in writing.

This new rule represents a very significant change in practice and means the solicitor must be even more careful to ensure his client-testator's will is properly and legally executed.

For further detailed discussion of the formalities for making a valid will, please refer to the standard text books referred to in Chapter 10, 'Further Reading'.

2.5 Modes of revocation

A will may be revoked in four ways:

(a) by physical destruction;

(b) by a subsequent will or codicil with an intent to revoke;

(c) by marriage;

(d) by divorce or annulment of an existing marriage.

By s 20 of the Wills Act 1837, a will may be revoked by 'burning, tearing or otherwise destroying the same by the testator, or by some person in his presence and by his direction, with the intention of revoking the same'. Two points are very important: first, the destruction must be by the testator himself or by some other person in his presence by his direction (see, in particular, *Re Dodds* (1857) Dea & SW 290 on this point); and second, physical destruction must be effected – note *Cheese v Lovejoy* (1877) 2 PD 251, where it was held that merely writing 'revoked' across a will is not sufficient to revoke the will. However, the obliteration of a signature may revoke a will (see *In Re the Estate of Adams (Deceased)* [1990] Ch 601).

Section 20 of the 1837 Act also provides for revocation of a will by a later will or codicil.

Normally, one of the first clauses inserted in a professionally drafted will declares that the testator revokes all former wills and testamentary dispositions made previously (see standard clause suggested at 5.2) – so that the new will makes it clear that it alone is to contain all the testator's wishes as to the disposition of his property on death. A will may, however, be destroyed without express revocation of this kind (or any reference to revocation) if the later will in time contradicts the former will and deals with the totality of the testator's estate.

Revocation is usually automatic on the marriage of the testator (s 18 of the Wills Act 1937) or on the dissolution or annulment of a subsisting marriage (s 18A of the Wills Act 1837, inserted by s 18 of the Administration of Justice Act 1982).

The decision in *Re Sinclair* [1985] 1 All ER 1066 has been overruled by the Law Reform (Succession) Act 1995, which became operative in law on 1 January 1996. As and from that date, property left by will to a former spouse will devolve as if the former spouse had died on the date of divorce/annulment of marriage. Where a spouse whose marriage has been dissolved or annulled is appointed as executor or trustee of the other spouse's will, the provision will take effect as if the former had predeceased him. Thus, *Re Sinclair* is nullified and former spouses' entitlements negated. Revocation by marriage is subject to statutory exceptions. A will or disposition in a will expressly made in contemplation of marriage to a particular person in reliance on s 177 of the Law of Property Act 1925, is not revoked by marriage to that person (see s 18(3) and (4) of the Wills Act 1837, as substituted by s 18(1) of the Administration of Justice Act 1982). For a standard clause to give effect to the 'in contemplation of marriage' exception, see 5.3.

The other exception is in s 18(2) of the Wills Act 1837 (as substituted by s 18(1) of the Administration of Justice Act 1982), whereby the general rule is that the exercise of a power of appointment in a pre-nuptial will continues to remain effective after the marriage, even where the remainder of the will is revoked.

Consideration should be given to the doctrine of conditional revocation, that is, where the testator intends the revocation of his will to take effect only if some condition is fulfilled. For a decision on the doctrine see *Re Carey* (1977) 121 Sol Jo 173, but see, also, *Re Jones* [1976] Ch 200, which should be distinguished from it.

2.6   Republication and revival of wills

A will may be republished by re-execution of the original will or a subsequent codicil, that is, the will is treated as referring to events not at the original date of the will, but at the date of subsequent re-execution, or at the date of the later codicil as the case may be. Republication has the effect of making the will speak or be deemed to take effect from the date of re-execution or the codicil. Revival is covered by s 22 of the Wills Act 1837 and occurs either by re-execution of the revoked instrument, or the execution of a codicil showing an intention to revive.

2.7   Law of intestacy

The rules as to devolution of the estate of a person dying without having made a will are to be found in Pt IV of the Administration of Estates Act 1925 (as amended) and provide for the distribution of the deceased person's estate according to set rules among his kin, which may or may not give effect to the wishes of the testator (see Chapter 1).

By s 33(1) of the 1925 Act, all the property, both real and personal, of the deceased person is held by his personal representatives on trust for sale with a power to postpone sale and so notionally converted into money.

The surviving spouse (whether widow or widower) has the primary right to the deceased's estate and is entitled to:

(a) all the personal chattels of the deceased as defined by s 55 of the Act;

(b) a fixed sum with interest which is £125,000 plus certain interest thereon at the rate of 6% from the date of death until the date of payment if the deceased is survived by issue (children, grandchildren, etc), or £200,000 where the deceased is survived only by certain specified relatives; and

(c) life interest in half of the residue estate where there are issue, or an absolute interest in half the residue where the deceased is survived only by the 'specified relatives'.

The 'specified relatives' for this purpose are parents or brothers or sisters of the whole blood or their issue who attain 18 or marry under that age.

Personal chattels are defined by s 55(1)(x) of the 1925 Act and include, broadly speaking, articles of household or personal use or ornament, such as clothes, furniture, jewellery, motor cars and domestic animals. The definition does not, however, include any article used by the deceased at the time of his death for business purposes, nor does it include money or securities (for example, stocks and shares).

To determine whether an asset is used for personal or business purposes, the article is to be classified according to the main purpose to which it is put at the date of the intestate's death – see *Re MacCulloch's Estate* (1981) 44 NSR (2nd) 666; this was a case decided in Nova Scotia on similar words to those of s 55(1)(x) and, in the absence of any English authority on the point, it is very strong persuasive authority.

The surviving spouse has, in addition, two personal rights:

(a) to elect to capitalise his or her life interest under s 47(A)(3) of the Act; and

(b) to elect to take the matrimonial home (providing he or she was residing there at the date of death) in satisfaction of the whole or part of his or her entitlement under the estate (Sched 2, para 1(1) of the Intestates Estates Act 1952).

Where the value of the matrimonial home is greater than the rights under the estate, the surviving husband or wife is entitled to make up any shortfall in the purchase price from his or her own resources (*Re Phelps* [1980] Ch 275).

The spouse takes the whole estate if there are no issue or relatives as specified above who survive the deceased.

Where a person dies intestate, but is not survived by his or her spouse, the whole estate passes to the issue equally (grandchildren taking their parents' share equally between them if the parent predeceases the intestate).

Where the deceased is not survived by a spouse or issue, then the estate passes:

(a) to the deceased's parents equally if both are surviving;

(b) if the deceased's parents are dead, to his brothers or sisters of whole blood and their issue equally;

(c) in the event of no relatives in (a) and (b) surviving the deceased, to the brothers and sisters of the half-blood and their issue, or if there are none, to the deceased's grandparents equally;

(d) where there are none of the relatives in the above categories surviving the deceased, the estate passes to aunts and uncles of the whole blood or their issue or, if none, to aunts and uncles of the half-blood or their issue. If there are none of these relatives, the law provides that the deceased's property passes to the Crown Duchy of Lancaster or Duchy of Cornwall, as the case may be, *in bona vacantia*.

If the property passes to the Crown *in bona vacantia* under s 46(1)(iv) of the 1925 Act, the Crown has a discretion to make payments according to the rules that have evolved over the years (see (1987) 84 Gazette 42, 3315). In this article on *ex gratia* payments, it is suggested that the Treasury Solicitor and the Solicitors for the Duchies of Lancaster and Cornwall, acting on behalf of the Crown, may make such payments under s 46(1)(iv) in the following circumstances:

(a) where the applicant (not usually an employee of the deceased) has performed essential services or substantial acts of kindness for the deceased without payment. The services are usually of a domestic nature;

(b) where the deceased person was of illegitimate birth, but survived by blood relatives, it is normally the practice to recommend the bar of illegitimacy be ignored;

(c) where the deceased left a testamentary document which was not valid as a will (for example, the statutory requirements of s 9 of the Wills Act 1837 (as amended) had not been complied with) or the deceased was actively engaged in making a will but died before formal execution of the will, providing the will or document or instructions represents the deceased's final testamentary intentions;

(d) in cases where there have been long periods of close association between the deceased and applicant, for example, where the deceased was brought up by the applicant as his own child;

(e) where the deceased has made a home for the applicant for many years, for example, a lodger who shares in the family life.

The article emphasises that such payments are purely discretionary and not as of right, and, in addition, considers the interrelationship of *ex gratia* payments and claims under the family provision legislation.

It will be obvious from this outline of the intestacy rules that they do not always give effect to the deceased person's wishes as to the disposition of his property on death; see 1.2.

For deaths on or after 1 January 1996, s 1(2) of the Law Reform (Succession) Act 1995 has abolished the hotchpotch rules and s 1(1) has introduced the concept of a 28 day survivorship clause between husband and wife on intestacy, that is, under the law of intestacy where the intestate's spouse dies within 28 days of the intestate, the estate is distributed as if the spouse had not survived the intestate.

2.8   Family provision on death

Under s 1 of the Inheritance (Provision for Family and Dependants) Act 1975, the court has power to make reasonable financial provision, by way of either capital or income, out of the estate of a person who dies testate or intestate, and hence effectively limits the freedom of a deceased person to leave his estate to whomsoever he wishes by his will.

By s 1(1) of this Act, the persons entitled to claim are listed as:

(a) the spouse;

(b) a former spouse who has not remarried;

(c) a child;

(d) a child of the family (for example, a stepchild);

(e) certain other dependants of the deceased for example, mistresses (*Malone v Harrison* [1979] 1 WLR 1353) and distant relatives.

By s 1(2) of the Act, the spouse is entitled to a higher standard of provision than all other potential claimants. This is known as the 'surviving spouse' standard.

By s 4, all applications for financial provision must be made not later than six months after the grant of representation to the estate, although the period can be extended with leave of court if certain defined guidelines apply (*Re Salmon* [1981] Ch 167).

As was stated in Chapter 1, under s 21 of the 1975 Act, the deceased may make a written or oral statement as to why he has not provided for a particular person in his will and this statement is considered along with the other guidelines for consideration by the court under s 3. (For a specimen clause in a will to give effect to s 21, see 5.25) The property out of which family provision can be ordered is defined as the 'net estate' under s 8 of the 1975 Act which provides, *inter alia*, for property to be claimed back under ss 10 and 11 where there are dispositions of property with an intention to defeat a family provision claim or contracts to leave property by will.

It should be noted that cohabitants have an added ground on which to claim (s 2 of the Law Reform (Succession) Act 1995), namely, if during the whole of the two year period ending immediately before the death of the deceased, the cohabitant was living in the same household as the deceased as his wife. This effectively amends s 1 of the 1975 statute. Recently, in the case of *Bouette v Rose* (2000) *The Times*, 1 February, it was established that a carer is entitled to bring a family provision claim.

The deceased (L) had suffered brain damage at birth as a result of medical negligence and received a large damages award in settlement for his injuries. His father left his mother eight months after L's birth and thereafter L was exclusively cared for by her mother. The damages awarded were used to keep L in a financial way that was necessary in the circumstances. L died without making a will (intestate). The Court of Appeal held that the mother was entitled to make a family provision claim against her daughter's estate.

2.9   Construction of wills

There are very complicated rules as to the construction of the words used in a will and the legal adviser is expected to understand and appreciate these rules when drafting a will (the courts are particularly hard on lawyers who fail to use words precisely). The drafter must, therefore, be extremely careful to use concise wording so as not to fall foul of the doctrine of construction of wills. (For a comprehensive account of the rules on construction of wills see, particularly, Mellows, *The Law of Succession*, Butterworths).

Exact and precise wording is particularly important, since rectification of a will is only possible in two circumstances, that is, either where there is a clerical error or a failure to understand the testator's instructions (see s 20 of the Administration of Justice Act 1982).

Application to the court is required for rectification even in these circumstances, and any such application might well raise a *prima facie* presumption of negligence on the part of a solicitor and will inevitably lead to an order for costs, probably against the negligent lawyer. In relation to cases of rectification of wills, the reader is recommended to study two recent cases on the point, namely, *Horsfall v Edwards* (1999) Lloyd's Rep 232, CA and *Walker v Medlicott and Son* (1998–99) 1 TELR 413.

2.10 Gifts by will

Different types of gift may be made under the provisions of a will and it is necessary to distinguish them.

A specific gift is a gift such as 'my car' or 'my house'. It is effectively a gift of specified items forming part of the deceased's estate, and it must have two characteristics: it must itself be part of the testator's personal or real property and it must be a specified part, so that it is severed or distinguished by the testator from the general mass of his estate. Generally, where the testator makes a specific gift, he uses the word 'my' or some other possessive word.

A general gift is a gift which is provided out of the testator's general estate. It is irrelevant whether its subject matter forms part of the testator's property at the time of his death, for example, 'a Rolls Royce car'. The gift is usually prefixed by the indefinite article. If the property referred to does not form part of the testator's estate at the time of his death, the personal representatives are under a legal duty to purchase an item of the type in question for the beneficiary or compensate the beneficiary by paying to him a sum of money representing the value of the item.

A pecuniary legacy is a gift of money, for example, '£1,000 to my friend William'.

A demonstrative legacy is a gift of a general, non-specific nature, directed to be paid out of a specific fund, for example, a gift of '£1,000 out of my account with Lloyds Bank'. If, on the death of the testator, there was only £500 in the account, the deficiency would have to be made good out of the general personal estate.

A residuary gift is what remains after payment of all debts, liabilities, expenses and other legacies.

The distinction between the different types of gift is very important for a number of reasons, for example, payment of interest, application of the doctrines of ademption (which only applies to specific gifts), abatement and the order of application of legacies, debts and liabilities of the estate.

Section 34(3) and Pt II of the First Schedule to the Administration of Estates Act 1925 sets out the order of application of the deceased's estate to meet funeral, testamentary and administration expenses, debts and liabilities (including Inheritance Tax under s 211 of the Inheritance Tax Act 1984) where the estate is solvent. The order of application is as follows:

(a) property undisposed of by the will (that is, subject to an intestacy), subject to retention thereout of a fund to satisfy pecuniary legacies;

(b) residuary property subject to the retention thereout of a fund to discharge any pecuniary legacies left by the deceased;

(c) property specifically given for the payment of debts;

(d) property specifically charged with the payment of debts;

(e) the pecuniary legacy fund;

(f) property the subject of a specific gift, rateably according to its value to the testator; and

(g) property appointed by will under a general power, rateably according to its value to the testator.

The word 'devise' is usually employed to refer to realty, whereas the word 'bequest' is used to denote a gift of personalty.

The order of the application of assets to meet debts is significant for two reasons:

(a) it includes liability to Inheritance Tax; and

(b) it has the effect of making the residuary estate liable if there is no undisposed of estate, and therefore, care should be taken not to make too many pecuniary legacies if the testator's paramount intention is to benefit the residuary legatee (see 4.4 for further comment on this situation).

Where the estate is insolvent, reference must be made to the insolvency rules.

2.11 *Donatio mortis causa* and nominations

2.11.1 *Donatio mortis causa*

A *donatio mortis causa* is a conditional gift made in contemplation of death which will only take effect if the donor actually dies.

The donor must hand dominion over the property to the donee in his lifetime and the gift must be one of pure personalty. On the death of the donor, the gift vests not in the deceased's personal representatives, but in the donee (see the effect of the rule in *Strong v Bird* (1874) LR 18 Eq 315, as explained in the standard text books).

A *donatio mortis causa* is subject to payment of the deceased's debts if there is a deficiency of assets and is liable to Inheritance Tax. It is thought that the transferor is not liable for the tax under s 199(1)(a) of the Inheritance Tax Act 1984, but rather that his personal representatives are liable under s 200(1)(a). In the recent decision of *Sen v Headley* [1991] Ch 425, CA, it was confirmed that a *donatio mortis causa* of land can be made by the mere delivery of the title deeds to the land by the donor in his lifetime and that such delivery would give the donee a legal or equitable interest in the property. It had always been thought that it was impossible to effect a *donatio mortis causa* of land unless a formal deed of conveyance is employed to convey the legal estate.

2.11.2 Nominations

Nominations are designed to allow less wealthy members of society to dispose of small amounts of money without the necessity of making a will or their personal representatives obtaining a grant.

In certain circumstances, the property will not vest in the nominator's personal representatives on death, but will be paid directly to the nominee. The payer therefore needs to see a death certificate, but will not require production of a grant of probate. In addition, the payer should see a copy of the nomination if he does not already have the actual nomination in his possession. However, the nominated property does form part of the deceased's estate for Inheritance Tax purposes.

Nominations can be made in respect of deposits in certain Trustee Savings Banks, Friendly Societies and Industrial and Provident Societies up to a limit of £5,000 each. It is not possible to nominate National Savings Certificates and deposits in National Savings Banks and Trustee Savings Banks as this power was withdrawn on 1 May 1979 in respect of the latter and in respect of the two former on 1 May 1981.

To be valid, a nomination must be:

(a) in writing;

(b) made by a person who is 16 and over;

(c) attested by one witness.

As a will cannot be made by a person who is under the age of 18, a nomination is the only way in which a minor can effectively dispose of his property on death, unless he has the benefit of privileged status.

A nomination can be revoked by subsequent marriage, a later nomination or the death of the nominee before the nominator, but it is not revoked by a subsequent will. It is therefore advisable when drafting a will for a client to ascertain whether he has made any previous nominations. A separate and distinct form of nomination in respect of benefits under occupational pensions can be made.

One leading case relating to nominations is *Baird v Baird* [1990] AC 548, PC. It dealt with a nomination by a member of a company pension scheme of a beneficiary, to receive the death benefit payable under the scheme on the member's death before retirement. The Privy Council held that this was not a testamentary disposition by the member and so the nomination was valid despite non-compliance with the statutory requirements for a will.

However, it is not the court's decision which was so important, so much as the discussion in the Privy Council by the Law Lords of what a nomination actually is, and what its characteristics are.

It was also suggested by the Law Lords (in particular, Lord Oliver) that it is unlikely that the provision of the Wills Act 1837 would apply to nominations under modern pension schemes. He did, however, make one caveat to this statement, namely, that the question depended in each case on the provisos of the individual scheme.

This is a very important case, not only in respect of nominations relating to pension schemes, but also with regard to nominations generally, and the reader would be well advised to study it.

2.12 Powers of attorney and the Court of Protection

Frequently, a client enquires about powers of attorney when consulting his solicitor over the drafting of his will.

The concept of the enduring power of attorney (other powers of attorney are revoked by mental incapacity) was introduced by s 1 of the Enduring Powers of Attorney Act 1985. Previously, a power of attorney was revoked by the supervening mental incapacity of the donor and this still applies in the case of an ordinary power of attorney. However, an enduring power will not be revoked in these circumstances.

On 31 July 1990, a further set of regulations came into force prescribing a new form of enduring power of attorney (see the Enduring Powers of Attorney (Prescribed Form) Regulations 1990 SI 1990/1376). The Regulations are supplemented by a pamphlet produced by the Public Trust Office which is readily available to solicitors, citizens' advice bureaux and casual enquirers. The pamphlet is intended to clarify many of the matters upon which doubts have been expressed in the past. For a comprehensive treatment of the subject of enduring powers of attorney, refer to Aldridge, *Powers of Attorney*, Sweet & Maxwell.

A power of attorney, even an enduring one, is automatically revoked by operation of law on the death of the donor, and therefore a will is required to deal with the devolution of the donor's estate on death.

The execution of an enduring power of attorney avoids the necessity to apply to the Court of Protection in the case of mental incapacity. This court is expensive and cumbersome.

In 1996, revised guidelines on enduring powers of attorney were issued by the Law Society's Health and Disability Committee. A copy of these revised guidelines can be obtained from The Policy Directorate, The Law Society, 113 Chancery Lane, London WC1A 1PL (DX 56 London/Chancery Lane).

3 Taking the Client's Instructions

3.1 Introduction

In preparing a will, it cannot be emphasised enough that great care must be exercised in taking precise, detailed instructions. This will save time and trouble later and will ensure that the will accords fully with the client's wishes and circumstances. As a prelude to giving any legal advice and drafting the will, the practitioner must obtain all the client's financial and personal details.

Full and detailed instructions should be taken on the following points. (Note that, if the client turns out to have property abroad, special problems may arise, consideration of which is beyond the scope of this book.)

Some elderly people are entitled to 'green form' legal advice and assistance to make a will, for example, if they are over 70 or suffer from some incapacity (for example, deafness or dumbness) or a mental disorder, or congenital deformity, and this must be borne in mind.

3.2 Personal details

Ask the client for:

(a) name(s);

(b) address;

(c) telephone numbers at home and work;

(d) marital status or occupation and if married, client's maiden name;

(e) age;

(f) nationality;

(g) domicile;

(h) confirmation that England is the client's country of residence for tax purposes.

Where the client has been previously married, ask for details of previous name and the financial and personal circumstances (if known) of previous partner (so as to advise on a possible family provision claim).

Take detailed instructions as to the living relatives of the testator, particularly the full name of his wife and the full names and ages of his children and grandchildren, together with their full addresses, in order that advice can be given as to the clauses to be inserted in the will, for example, guardianship clauses, and the tax planning considerations taken into account. Ask tactfully if the client is living with anyone else.

3.3 Financial details

(a) Details of the address and estimated value of any real property owned should be taken from the client together with details of mortgages or charges on the property and where the deeds to the property are kept.

(b) Ascertain from the client whether such real property and any personal property forming part of estate is held in joint/single names of the client and spouse.

(c) Ask the client for details of any bank or building society and Post Office accounts held, together with the name of the bank or building society, amount in each account and details of the tax district (with reference, if possible), or client's National Insurance number.

(d) Request details of assurance/insurance policies held by the client.

(e) Request details of any occupational or other pension rights to which your client may be entitled including whether the pension makes provision for the widow/widower and dependants (and if there are death-in-service benefits).

(f) Obtain details of any stocks/shares held by the client and their approximate value (and ask for address of his accountant/stockbroker, if appropriate).

(g) Request details of all mortgages, hire purchase agreements or other substantial debts owed by the client.

(h) Request details of any specific chattels of significant value and request instructions as to their disposal on death, that is, whether they are to be the subject of specific gifts or to be sold.

(i) Request details of any interests the client may have under trusts or settlements with details of the trust or settlement, for example, name and date of trust; name and address of trustees; nature of testator's interest; estimated value of his interest.

(j) Request details of the financial circumstances of spouse so as to be able to advise as to possible equalisation of estates (see 4.3).

NB: suggest to the client that for the purposes of tax planning it may be appropriate for both spouses to make wills at the same time.

3.4 Testator's wishes

(a) Ask client if he wishes to make any pecuniary legacies to charities or relatives.

(b) Ask client if he wishes to make any bequests of particular personal effects.

(c) Ask client to whom he wishes the residue of his estate to pass.

(d) Ask client whom he wishes to be his executors. Advice at this time should be given on:

- the effect of legacies on the residuary estate;
- Inheritance Tax implications of absolute or life interests, particularly in the matrimonial home;
- the type of executor to appoint;
- the possible need for substitution executors/trustees.

(e) Request the client's instructions as to mode of burial/cremation and any specific wishes as to church.

(f) Ask the client if he wishes any part(s) of his body to be utilised after his death for medical research.

(g) Ascertain details of any gifts made by the client in the last seven years and remind him of the Inheritance Tax implications (see 4.3).

(h) Take details of client's entitlement under any trusts or settlements and remind him of the implications of such interests.

(i) Ask client whether he has made a previous will and where it can be found, and specifically whether he has made a will in a foreign jurisdiction relating to property within that jurisdiction, for example, if he owns a flat in Spain.

(j) Confirm that he wishes all previous wills to be treated as revoked.

3.5 Safe deposit of will

(a) Ascertain whether the testator wishes to keep his original will or leave it with you, also whether he wishes to keep a copy.

(b) Advise as to the procedure available at the Principal Probate Registry for the safe keeping of wills (see Wills (Deposit for Safe Custody) Regulations 1978 SI 1978/1724), referred to in more detail at 4.7).

(c) Inform client of the existence of the Law Society's Personal Assets Log which includes details of, *inter alia*, the client's solicitor, his will and the executors/trustees of the will, and ask the client if he wishes to keep one.

3.6   Exclusion of apportionment rules

Ask client, after explaining the apportionment rules in simple terms, whether he wishes the rules in *Howe v Earl of Dartmouth* (1802) 7 Ves 137, *Allhusen v Whittell* (1867) LR 4 Eq 295 and *Re Earl of Chesterfield's Trust* (1883) 24 Ch D 643 to be excluded. These rules are invariably excluded in modern wills.

3.7   Confirmatory letter to client

Send a letter to client thanking him for his instructions and confirming them in detail, and enclose draft will for approval. Do not forget to include in your letter the details required by the 'client care' regime (see r 15 of Solicitors' Practice Rules 1990).

Do not forget the golden rule of Templeman J in *Re Simpson* (1977) 121 Sol Jo 224 (see Chapter 2) concerning the precautionary need for medical advice if the testator is illiterate, elderly or seriously ill, but be very careful not to imply lack of capacity through age, as to mention or even imply senility may be offensive and lead to the client going to another solicitor.

3.8   Checklist

Date of instructions;

Client's full name, address and occupation;

Telephone numbers:
- home;
- business;
- mobile number (if any);

Client's age and place of domicile;

Residence for tax purposes (tax reference number) plus details of any accountant they employ;

Relatives' details:

- names;
- addresses and telephone numbers;
- ages (any under 18);

Name and address of person to be contacted on death;

Names and address(es) of executor/trustees and substitute executor/trustees;

Details of any person with whom the client is living;

Details of pecuniary legacies:

- legatee's name and address;
- amount of legacy;

Details of specific legatees:

- legatee's name and address;
- chattel(s) involved;

Details of residuary legatee(s):

- legatee's name;
- address;
- telephone number;

Details of any realty owned and:

- whether free of mortgage or otherwise;
- whether in joint or single names;
- where deeds are kept;
- details of any foreign property;

Details of bank/building society/Post Office accounts:

- name of bank/building society;
- address;
- account number;
- type of account;

Details of pension rights:

- name of company;
- address of company;
- reference number;

- whether pension rights/death-in-service benefits nominated or written in trust;

Details of life assurance policies:

- name of company;
- address of company;
- account number;
- value of policy;
- whether policies written in trust or not;

Details of shares/stocks;

Details of interests under trust/settlements:

- name and date of trust;
- names and addresses of trustees;

Cremation/transplant of parts of body:

- details;
- carry donor card?;

Is original will to be kept by us or deposited with Principal Probate Registry?;

Details of debts, hire-purchase agreements;

- name of debtor/hire-purchase company;
- address of debtor/hire-purchase company;

Details of former spouse or other possible family provision claimant;

Details of accountant/stockbroker – name, address and telephone number;

Inheritance Tax advice:

- on death;
- details of lifetime gifts:

(1) date made;

(2) beneficiary/beneficiaries;

Location of last will;

Confirmatory letter:

- request any further information;
- thank client for his instructions;
- include any points relevant to the execution of the will (see 4.9).

4 Advising the Client

4.1 Appointment of executors and trustees

When taking instructions for a will (Chapter 3), the wishes of the testator with regard to the persons who will administer his estate (the executors) and who will act as trustees of any trust established under the terms of his will must be ascertained. Often, a testator will appoint the same person to hold both offices.

Any number of executors may be appointed, but no more than four can take out a grant in respect of the same property (s 114(1) of the Supreme Court Act 1981). It is advisable to appoint not less than two executors in case one of them predeceases the testator or dies before completion of the administration of the estate. If the executors are also to be the trustees, it is essential to appoint two, but not more than four trustees, since two are required (except in case of the trust corporation) to give a valid receipt for capital moneys under s 27 of the Law of Property Act 1925.

The testator may appoint as executor an individual, a firm of solicitors, a bank, a trustee corporation or the public trustee. Individuals may be relatives or friends. They have the advantage that they may be persons in whom the testator has confidence and they are unlikely to charge a fee for acting. Normally, where a sole executor is appointed, a substitutional appointment should be incorporated in the will.

It is frequently advisable to appoint professional advisers (such as solicitors or accountants) who will be experts in administering the estates of deceased persons and drawing up the necessary accounts and other pertinent documents. They will, of course, normally charge for their services. When appointing a solicitor or accountant as executor, it is more practical to appoint the firm rather than an individual who may predecease the testator or leave the firm. An appointment of a firm of solicitors is normally construed as an appointment of the partners in the firm at the date of the will.

Some testators prefer to appoint their bankers as executors of their will. Banks usually insist that their own standard form of appointment clause is inserted in the will and, if required, this may be obtained from the relevant bank on application. However, it should be mentioned that the fees charged by banks to act are often higher than where a solicitor or firm of solicitors is appointed, for example, where conveyancing is involved and the bank has to instruct independent solicitors to act in the conveyance. The public trustee may, in limited circumstances, be appointed. For when this is advisable or necessary, refer to the standard works listed in Chapter 10.

4.2   Common/standard clauses

There are certain standard clauses which ought to be inserted in a will, as well as special clauses appropriate to a client's own personal and financial circumstances, and these should be brought to the client's attention.

The common or standard clauses are listed below, together with a number of special clauses which should be inserted in a will in the appropriate circumstances. The list is not an exhaustive one – for example, there are special clauses which are required in drafting the wills of farmers. (Precedents of most of the clauses referred to here appear in full accompanied by an explanatory comment as to their effect in Chapter 5, 'Precedent Clauses'.)

- Commencement of will and revocation clause.
- Commencement of will in contemplation of marriage.
- Clause(s) dealing with funeral wishes and any statement as to use of the deceased's body or parts thereof after death for transplant.
- Appointment of executors and trustees and substitution executors/trustees.
- Appointment of testamentary guardians of minor children.
- Absolute gift of house or gift of life interest in house.
- Gift of house free of mortgage.
- Absolute gift of specific chattels.
- Gifts of pecuniary legacies.
- Gifts to charities, clubs and societies.
- Gifts of residue subject to 28 day survivorship clause.
- Gift to wife, with gift over to issue.
- Gift of residue on trust for sale.

- Incorporating protective trusts or deferring the vesting of the beneficiary's interest until a specified age is attained.

- Accruer clause.

- Extension of powers of maintenance and advancement under ss 31 and 32 of the Trustee Act 1925.

- Extension of powers of investment.

- Power to appropriate without consents.

- Powers in relation to carrying on a business of a deceased person.

- Power to insure.

- Exclusion of apportionment rules, for example, under *Howe v Earl of Dartmouth* (1802) 7 Ves 137 and *Allhusen v Whittell* (1867) LR 4 Eq 295.

- Executors' and trustees' charging clause.

- Receipts by minors.

- Power of appointment of a new trustee.

- Witness clause.

- 'Signed by the testator in our presence' clause.

- Declaration by testator as to why no provision has been made for a particular person under s 21 of the Inheritance (Provision for Family and Dependants) Act 1975.

- The clauses above are of cause subject to the changes and amendments: refer to the discussion of the Trustee Act 2000 (see Chapter 7).

4.3   Inheritance Tax planning

By virtue of s 136 of the Finance Act 1986, as updated annually thereafter by delegated legislation (and most recently by SI 2000/803), for transfers on or after 6 April 2000, Inheritance Tax has only two rates; a nil band rate for chargeable transfers up to £234,000, and thereafter a 40% rate.

Advise client to take advantage, where appropriate, of the potentially exempt transfer rules relating to gifts made seven years before death (s 3A(1) of the Inheritance Tax Act 1984).

Potentially exempt transfers have been defined as 'specific sorts of transfers of value which escape an Inheritance Tax charge if the transferor survives the making of them by seven years' (Lyons, *Chapman's Inheritance Tax*, Sweet & Maxwell, p 13).

However, if the transferor dies within the seven year period, reduced rates of Inheritance Tax are paid as follows in accordance with s 7(4) of the Inheritance Tax Act 1984:

Transfer made	Rate of charge
Up to 3 years before death	death rates
Over 3 years and not more than 4 years	80% of death rates
Over 4 and not more than 5 years	60% of death rates
Over 5 and not more than 6 years	40% of death rates
Over 6 and not more than 7 years	20% of death rates

Advise client as to other possible exemptions and reliefs (these are clearly explained in *Chapman's Inheritance Tax*, Chapter 5, pp 77 *et seq*). These include the following (all references here are to the Inheritance Tax Act 1984):

(a) The £234,000 nil band rate – tax is only leviable where the cumulative total value of chargeable transfers made in the lifetime and on death is in excess of £234,000. Up to that limit, tax-free gifts can be made irrespective of whether any specific exemption is available, but it must be remembered that the availability of such an exemption is not without importance, because gifts which are specifically exempted are not included in the cumulative total of £200,000.

(b) Transfers between spouses – they are totally exempt from a levy to tax (s 18) unless the donee spouse is domiciled outside the UK when the exemption is limited to £55,000.

(c) Every taxpayer is allowed an annual tax free allowance of £3,000 (s 19).

(d) Small gifts to the same person – there is a general exemption from Inheritance Tax of £250 per donee, and a donor can make gifts to as many donees as he wishes provided each individual gift does not exceed £250.

(e) Gifts in consideration of marriage are exempt transfers with limits which range from £5,000 to £1,000 depending on the relationship between donor and donee (s 22):

   • a £5,000 exemption limit applies to a parent of a party to a marriage if either an outright gift is made to either party to the marriage, or a settled gift is made and the class of beneficiaries is restricted to: parties or issue of the marriage; or a spouse of such issue; or a subsequent spouse of a party to the marriage; or any issue or spouse of such issue of a subsequent marriage of either; or as respects a reasonable amount of remuneration, the trustees of the settlement (s 22(4));

- a £2,500 limit applies to gifts by a party to a marriage and gifts by grandparents or remoter ancestors of either party to the marriage if the gift is either an outright gift to the other or either party to the marriage, or a settled gift and the class of beneficiaries is restricted as above;

- a £1,000 limit applies to gifts by another person (for example, uncle, aunt, brother, sister, employer, etc) if the gift is either outright to either party to the marriage or a settled gift and the class of beneficiaries is restricted as above. 'Child' includes an illegitimate, adopted or stepchild (s 22(2)).

(f) Gifts treated as normal expenditure out of income (s 21). Gifts will be exempt from tax in so far as:

- they are shown to be made as part of the normal expenditure of the transferor;

- they are made out of income;

- that, after allowing for transfers of value forming part of his normal expenditure, the transferor is left with sufficient income to maintain his usual high standard of living (see the illuminating case of *Bennett v IRC* [1995] STC 54).

(g) Dispositions for maintenance of the family – a disposition by one party to the marriage for the maintenance, education or training of a child of either spouse is not a transfer of value, nor is financial provision after the breakdown of the marriage when the parties are divorced (s 11).

(h) A transfer of value during the lifetime or on death to a charity does not give rise to a charge for Inheritance Tax (s 23(1)).

(i) Gifts for national purposes (for example, to the British Museum and National Gallery) are not chargeable to tax (s 25(1) and Third Schedule).

(j) Gifts to certain public bodies, if the Inland Revenue so directs before or at the time of the gift, are also not chargeable to tax (s 26).

(k) Transfers in the course of business may also be exempt from Inheritance Tax, for example, gratuities paid to employees or their dependants (s 12(1)).

(l) Quick succession relief is also available where a recipient of property dies within five years of the chargeable event which increased the value of his estate (s 141). The scale rates are as follows (s 141(3)):

Periods between first and second chargeable transfers	Tax credit available on second transfer, as a percentage of the tax on first transfer
1 year or less	100%
Between 1 and 2 years	80%
Between 2 and 3 years	60%
Between 3 and 4 years	40%
Between 4 and 5 years	20%
More than 5 years	NIL

Advice should be given as to equalisation of spouses' estates up to the nil band rate of £234,000 (plus, possibly, as circumstances demand, the value of two annual exemptions, that is, £6,000).

In the example of a couple, worth between them £600,000, who have failed to make lifetime gifts, a considerable saving in the Inheritance Tax levy can be effected. Were all the property to devolve on the surviving spouse, who then left all his estate to the children, no tax is payable on the first death by virtue of the spouse exemption, but on the death of the second spouse, there is a potential liability to a substantial tax charge, that is, £366,000 at 40%, or an Inheritance Tax liability of £146,400.

If the estates of the spouses are equalised so that each spouse has an estate valued at £300,000 and the first spouse leaves his estate to the children, there is a substantially reduced inheritance bill, that is, on the death of each spouse £66,000 x 40% or £26,400 on each death x 2 = £52,800 – a net saving of 64% or £93,600. (Inter-spousal transfers are free of Inheritance Tax and Capital Gains Tax, but when making inter-spousal transfers, attention must be paid to any potential Income Tax considerations.)

All practitioners must be careful to remember that, on all occasions, attention must be given to the interrelationship of all three personal taxes, that is, Income Tax, Capital Gains Tax and Inheritance Tax.

A solicitor must, in addition, consider whether one spouse would be better leaving the other a life interest or an absolute interest. If a life interest is conferred upon the surviving spouse, as she cannot alienate the property, the children are bound on the second death to inherit the capital in specie. Gifts, whether absolute or of a life interest, in the income are covered by the spouse exemption on first death but liable to Inheritance Tax on the second death – the Inheritance Tax position will be the same. If a life interest is conferred by the first spouse on the second spouse, obviously a larger fund may be essential so that the income is sufficient to meet the second spouse's living requirements (account would have to be taken of the second spouse's own income and capital resources).

In this situation, as an alternative to conferring an interest in income for life on the surviving spouse, it might be prudent by will to establish a mini-discretionary trust.

The husband creates a mini-discretionary trust of the nil band rate at the date of his death less the value of:

(a) any potentially exempt transfers (PETS);

(b) lifetime chargeable transfers;

(c) gifts in his will or any codicil;

(d) any gifts in breach of the reservation of benefit rules;

(e) any benefits in settled property by way of interest in possession in favour of a class of named beneficiaries, for example, spouse, children and remoter issue.

On the death of the husband, the trustees then have up to two years (excluding the first three months in favour of a surviving spouse) to determine whether to appoint property representing the nil band rate to the children or the spouse depending on financial and personal circumstances. Hence, the maximum flexibility is achieved and, in addition, the trustees may appoint all or any part of the nil band rate to the discretionary objects under s 144 of the Inheritance Tax Act 1984. The testator usually signs a letter of wishes, which is not legally binding on his trustees, indicating his wishes as to the distribution of nil band rate under the trust (see precedent of nil band rate legacy will, 6.4).

This book is not intended to be a treatise on tax planning, and reference should normally be made to larger texts (for example, *Tolley's Estate Planning*). However, the following outline points should, in addition, be borne in mind and, in respect of these, it would be prudent to take specialist advice, for example, of counsel:

(a) The anti-avoidance sections in the Inheritance Tax Act 1984 (and elsewhere) and the implications of the decision in *IRC v Ramsay* [1982] AC 300.

(b) The advantage of effecting in trust arrangements for life assurance policies and death-in-service benefits of personal pensions.

(c) Nomination in case of rights under occupational pensions.

(d) Asset freezing, asset reduction and asset conversion, for example, by use of annual exemptions, business relief, etc.

(e) The decision in *Ingram v Inland Revenue Commissioners* [1995] STC 564 on carving out interests in property as nullified by s 104 of the Finance Act 1999.

(f) As to the tax planning opportunities where there is a married couple, refer to Whitehouse, *Revenue Law – Principles and Practices*, Butterworths, which includes a very useful chapter on tax planning for the family unit.

(g) The wise solicitor should advise his clients of the possible use of Deeds of Variation and Deeds of Disclaimer on a deceased's death, more details of which can be found in White, *Post-Death Rearrangements of Wills and Intestacies*, Longman.

(h) It must be emphasised that there are many ways of avoiding or mitigating Inheritance Tax and the reader is particularly referred to two works on estate planning: *Estate Planning*, Tolley; and *Ray's Practical Inheritance Tax Planning*, Butterworths.

(i) Use can also be made of accumulation and maintenance settlements whereby income is accumulated for minor beneficiaries for a period of time. A discretionary trust can also be established. This allows for the money to be paid into a discretionary trust up to the nil band rate, and means that the settlor can determine in what shares and which beneficiaries should take at a later date.

The other form of settlement available is a life in possession settlement which gives the life tenant an immediate right to the income and preserves the property in the family. The disadvantage of this is that on the death of the life tenant, the whole of the assets forming the settlement are liable to Inheritance Tax.

4.4 Form of gifts

A solicitor advising on a will must be extremely careful to ensure that the client appreciates that any gifts of pecuniary legacies will result in a reduction of the size of the residuary estate.

Frequently, the testator wishes to benefit a 'pet' charity by giving a legacy to it, but nevertheless, the overall objective is to provide substantially for, say, his children. If this is the position, it must be made absolutely clear that, because pecuniary legacies are paid first, they reduce the residue available for the residuary beneficiary and if, for example, the estate is very small because the testator survives for a number of years after execution of the will, it may be that although the legacies are paid in full, there is very little left for the residuary beneficiary. Clearly, this is not what the testator really intended and, therefore, he should be advised to keep pecuniary legacies to a minimum and to review the size of them or even omit them if he lives to a ripe old age. He should be strongly advised to see his solicitor occasionally to review the size of his estate and the effect on the provisions of his will, and he should be encouraged to review the provisions of the will himself as personal and financial circumstances alter.

4.5   Property subject to a charge

Section 35 of the Administration of Estates Act 1925 provides that if the testator leaves any interest in real or personal property by his will to someone (for example, a specific gift) and that property is charged with the payment of money, whether by way of legal mortgage, equitable charge or otherwise (including a lien for unpaid purchase money), and the deceased has not by will, deed or other document signified a contrary intention, the interest so charged shall, as between the different persons claiming through the deceased, be primarily liable for payment of the charge; and every part of the said interest, according to its value, shall bear a proportionate part of the charge on the whole thereof.

The client should be advised of the effect of this section and particularly if he makes a gift of specific property, for example, the matrimonial home, he should be asked whether he wishes the home to bear the cost of any charge (for example, building society mortgage) on it out of the value of the home itself, or whether he wishes the full value of the home to pass to the beneficiary and the mortgage to be discharged out of the general residuary estate.

4.6   Incidence of debts

Debts (including Inheritance Tax due under the provisions of s 211 of the Inheritance Tax Act 1984) are primarily paid out of the residuary estate and, in the appropriate circumstances, this should be emphasised to the client. The law on this subject is contained in s 34(3) and Pt II of the First Schedule to the Administration of Estates Act 1925. See 2.10 for exact details of the order of application of legacies, debts and liabilities of the estate.

4.7   Codicils and safe keeping of wills

Codicils change or amend part or parts of a will and can (and usually do) republish a will (that is, make it speak as property from the date of the codicil rather than the will). A client should here be advised to use codicils sparingly, since they may easily be lost and, in any case, are only really appropriate for minor amendments or changes to a will – it is preferable to incorporate substantial changes in a fresh will.

It is advisable to ask the testator if he has previously made a will, and if so, where it can be found. Generally, it should, where possible, be destroyed. (As to the valid means of revoking a will, see 2.5.)

It should also be drawn to the attention of the client that there is a provision for depositing a will for safe keeping with the Principal Probate Registry under the Wills (Deposit for Safe Custody) Regulations 1978 SI 1978/1724. The Principal Probate Registry is a registering authority regulated by ss 23–25 of the Administration of Justice Act 1982 and, as such, is obliged to provide and maintain depositories for the custody of wills of living persons. It is also the national body under the terms of the Convention on the Establishment of a Scheme of Registration of Wills (Registration Convention) (which was effected at Basle on 16 May 1972) for the purpose of arranging for the deposit of wills in other States privy to the Convention and of receiving and answering requests for information from the other States.

The circumstances under which a will may be deposited are regulated by the 1978 Regulations. Wills and codicils may be deposited on the personal attendance of the testator or by an agent authorised in writing at any District Probate Registry or Sub-Registry (for addresses of these registries, see Chapter 9). Where the will is registered at a District Probate Registry, it is sent on to the Principal Registrar in London for safe keeping. Alternatively, the testator may send his will by registered post direct to the Record Keeper at the Principal Probate Registry. Any will delivered or posted to the registry must be enclosed in a sealed envelope endorsed in the prescribed form (Form 22.1). A fee of £1.00 is payable on deposit. The registry then sends a certificate of deposit in the form prescribed by the regulations to the testator. A copy of the certificate is filed with the envelope containing the will.

The testator may, at any time, request the return of his will in writing, but must produce the certificate of deposit. A printed form of application can be obtained from the registry on request (Form 22.2). If the Registrar is satisfied as to the identity of the testator, the will is returned, but the testator must sign a receipt for it. In the form of receipt, the testator undertakes to notify his executor of withdrawal of the will from deposit at the registry. Otherwise, the will is retained by the registry until the testator dies.

A record is kept of all wills deposited pursuant to the regulations and a search is always made there before a grant is issued in respect of a deceased person.

On the death of the testator, application may be made to the Record Keeper at the Principal Registry for the sealed envelope containing the will to be opened and for the will to be passed on to the executor. Application is by prescribed form (Form 22.3). The Registrar will require to see a copy of the death certificate before handing over the will and he must be satisfied that the applicant is either the executor or some other person who intends to prove the will.

Before a deposited will is handed out, a copy is made and retained in the Principal Registry. The applicant must sign a receipt for the will and, if appropriate, give a written undertaking to lodge the will on any application for a grant of representation.

The prescribed forms are set out in the Regulations.

4.8 Execution of the will

It is essential that the client be reminded to inform the executor that he has made a will and where it can be found, or to leave a note to this effect somewhere easily accessible.

In the light of the decision of *Ross v Caunters* [1980] Ch 297, a solicitor must be very careful to advise a client on the exact method of execution and attestation of any will sent to the client for signature. It was held that a solicitor is liable if he fails to inform the testator that, if the will is witnessed by a beneficiary or the spouse of a beneficiary, that beneficiary remains a competent witness but loses his/her benefit (see s 15 of the Wills Act 1837). The liability in negligence is to the beneficiary. Note that the Court of Appeal held in *Clarke v Bruce Lance and Co (A Firm)* [1988] 1 All ER 364 that a solicitor who acted for a relation in preparing his will owed no duty of care to a beneficiary under that will when he subsequently acted in a transaction which effectively reduced the value of that beneficiary's interest under the will as previously drawn up.

It is recommended that the client be asked to attend the office to execute the will in order to ensure that mistakes are not made in its execution and attestation.

The issue of a solicitor's liability to intended beneficiaries has been substantially extended in recent years. In particular, take heed of the implications of the House of Lords' decision in *White v Jones* [1995]

2 WLR 187. This case was concerned with delay in preparation of a new will in accordance with the testator's instructions within a reasonable time. The effect of this was that the testator died before the new will was executed and the House of Lords held the solicitors liable in negligence to prospective beneficiaries under the will they had failed to prepare.

4.9   Advising the client: an *aide memoire*

- Advise clearly as to execution and attestation of the will and stress that the witnesses to the will must not be beneficiaries thereunder.

- Emphasise the considerable Inheritance Tax savings that can be effected by a skilfully drafted will and professional tax planning.

- Advise the client of the incidence of debts and legacies and the effect on the overall distribution of his estate.

- Ensure the client states clearly whether property given under the will is to be free or subject to charges, mortgages, etc subsisting at the date of death.

- Advise the client to review frequently the provisions of his will in the light of changes in his personal and financial circumstances.

- Advise as to safe keeping of the will.

- Remind the client to inform the executors where his will can be found, or to leave a note to this effect in an easily accessible place.

5 Precedent Clauses

5.1 Introduction

When preparing a will for a client, it is good practice to have in mind certain common/standard clauses for inclusion in the will in order to avoid serious omissions in its preparation. The Trusts of Land and Appointment of Trustees Act 1996, which became operative in law on 1 January 1997, made a number of changes to the clauses which need to be included in or excluded from a will precedent.

The Trustee Act 2000 (please refer to Chapter 7) makes it necessary for will drafters to reconsider the clauses they insert in a will.

Chapter 4 outlined the kinds of clauses that are frequently appropriate, depending on the individual circumstances of the client. In this chapter, precedents are suggested for most of those clauses. Commentary will be given on each clause, indicating its purpose and in what circumstances it would be advisable to include the clause.

The practitioner should not treat these clauses as exhaustive and is advised to refer to the appropriate volume of the *Encyclopaedia of Forms and Precedents*, Butterworths, and other precedent books such as Brighouse and George, *Precedents of Wills and Life Transfers*, Sweet & Maxwell. Refer also to Chapter 10 and, in particular, note the comprehensive looseleaf work *Practical Will Precedents*, Longman.

5.2 Commencement

A clause should be inserted at the start of the will as follows:

I [full name, address and occupation] HEREBY REVOKE all former Wills and testamentary dispositions made by me and DECLARE this to be my last Will.

The effect of such a clause is twofold – first, it clearly indicates that the present will is to be the testator's only effective will and, second, the words 'HEREBY REVOKE' are sufficient to express a clear intention to revoke all previous wills made by the testator (see s 20 of the Wills Act 1837).

It would be a sensible precaution to ensure that all previous wills made by the testator are destroyed (for example, by burning) so that confusion at a later date is avoided.

A practitioner would be well advised to ask a client whether he has any foreign property which devolved according to foreign law and, if so, to limit the revocation clause as follows:

> I hereby revoke all former Wills and testamentary dispositions hereto before made by me and declare this alone to be my last will and testament except that this will shall not revoke my Will in respect of my Spanish property made in Spain.

In this way, any will relating to foreign property is not inadvertently revoked – the foreign will is, of course, to remain valid so as to dispose of the testator's foreign property on his death.

NB: ensure the will is dated with the date of any actual execution either at the commencement or end of the will.

5.3 In contemplation of marriage

If the client is making a will with a view to marriage in the immediate future, a special provision must be included, since marriage will normally revoke a will (see s 18(1) of the Wills Act 1837, as substituted by s 18(1) of the Administration of Justice Act 1982).

Advantage must be taken of the exception to the normal rule as to revocation by marriage by including a clause declaring that the will is made expressly in contemplation of marriage and so benefit from the provisions of s 177 of the Law of Property Act 1925 (s 18 of the Wills Act 1837, as substituted by s 18(3) and (4) of the Administration of Justice Act 1982). Include a clause such as:

> I HEREBY make my Will this _____ day of 20__ which is conditional upon my intended marriage to [name of intended spouse] of [address] being SOLEMNISED within __ months of the date hereof and I declare that all my former Wills and testamentary dispositions shall not be revoked until solemnisation of the said marriage.

5.4 Funeral wishes

Clauses reflecting the testator's funeral wishes can be inserted, for example:

> I desire that my body be cremated and that my ashes be scattered [to the wind] [in the Garden of Remembrance at Crematorium]

or

> I desire that my body be buried in my parents' grave in the [_____ Cemetery] Parish Church of St [name and address] at [place].

There are, of course, many funeral wishes which may be contemplated and care should be exercised in taking precise instructions. It is advisable to make arrangements so that the nearest relatives of the deceased know exactly what the testator's funeral wishes are, as often the burial takes place before the will is found and therefore the testator's wishes may be inadvertently ignored.

Clauses may also be included requesting use of the deceased's body or parts of it for medical research/transplant operations. Many clauses exist to express such wishes, but an example is:

> I declare that it is my desire that after my death my [eyes] [kidneys] be used for therapeutic purposes.

Often, it is wise to advise the testator to carry a donor card on his person if he wishes to give parts of his body for medical purposes on his death.

The family of the deceased are not, in fact, legally bound by funeral and burial wishes except that a direction against cremation is effective in law – note, also, the previous comments at 1.2 on the legal position relating to the testator's wishes for the use of his body for medical research or transplant purposes.

5.5 Appointment of executors/trustees

All wills should include a provision appointing executors and substitute executors in those cases where a trust, corporation, or firm of solicitors has not been appointed in the first instance.

Where a sole executor dies and no substitute executorship clause has been included, the effect is to leave the deceased person's estate without an executor to administer and prove the will, unless the chain of representation applies (see s 7 of the Administration of Estates Act 1925). For the doctrine of the chain of representation and its exact effect refer to the standard works on wills, for example, Parry and Clark, *The Law of Succession*, Sweet & Maxwell.

A clause appointing an executor should read:

> I APPOINT my husband/wife to be sole Executor/Executrix of this my Will but if he/she shall predecease me or die without having proved my said Will I APPOINT _____ of _____ and _____ of _____ to be Executors/Trustees of this my Will and I declare that the expression 'my Trustees' used throughout this my Will shall where the context admits mean and include the Trustee or Trustees for the time being of this my Will whether original additional or substituted.

> It is often necessary to appoint trustees of a will in the form suggested above where the residuary estate is left on trust for sale and conversion.

If it is desired to appoint the partners of a firm as executors (see 4.1), the following clause may be inserted:

> I APPOINT [names, etc of partners] and _____ both of [address of partnership] being partners in the firm of [name of partnership] to be the Executors [and Trustees] of this my Will and if one of them shall predecease me or for any reason be unable or unwilling to act as Executor [and Trustee] I APPOINT the other partners at the date of my death in the firm of [name of partnership] or such other firm succeeding to the carrying on of its practice as Executors [and Trustees] in substitution but with the wish that no more than [two] persons shall prove my Will.

Reference in the clause should be made to any firm which succeeds to or takes over the firm's practice by amalgamation or otherwise.

5.6 Appointment of testamentary guardians

It is wise to provide for testamentary guardians of minor children and a clause appointing such guardians should always be inserted if applicable.

A suggested clause is:

> I APPOINT the said [specify person] and the said [specify person] to be guardians of any child of mine who may be a minor at the date of my death to act after the death of my wife jointly with any guardian or guardians appointed by my wife by Deed or Will.

If the deceased appoints guardians, they may act jointly with the surviving parent, or, if both parents are dead, and they have each appointed different sets of guardians, both sets may act jointly (see ss 3 and 4 of the Guardianship of Minors Act 1971).

5.7   Absolute gift of real estate

Where an absolute gift of the home is envisaged, this clause may be included:

> I GIVE (free of Inheritance Tax) any property in which I reside at the date of my death to [specify beneficiary] freed and discharged from any subsisting mortgage or charge for the time being affecting the property which I direct shall be discharged out of my residuary estate in exoneration of the said property.

This clause is fairly simple, but it should be made absolutely clear that the devise is to be free of any Inheritance Tax liability, and also it should be stated whether the property is given free or subject to mortgage or charge secured against the property (for example, a first charge to a building society); see s 35 of the Administration of Estates Act 1925. (The effect of s 35 is explained at 4.5.)

By employing the phrase 'any property in which I reside at the date of my death', the gift will cover any property owned by the deceased at the date of death – so preventing the necessity for amendment of the will if the deceased moves from one residence to another.

5.8   Specific gift of chattels

Clauses of specific gifts should be inserted where appropriate and a clause such as the following should be incorporated in the will:

> I GIVE to my said wife/husband _____ absolutely my personal chattels as defined by s 55(1)(x) of the Administration of Estates Act 1925 and also any motor car belonging to me even though used wholly or partly for business purposes

or

> I GIVE to _____ absolutely all of my chattels and effects of personal domestic or household use or ornament.

There is no need to include a 'free of tax' clause, as specific gifts are free of Inheritance Tax (see the discussion as to liability to Inheritance Tax at 5.9 below).

The phrase 'personal chattels as defined by s 55(1)(x) of the Administration of Estates Act 1925' is commonly understood by practitioners but should, if necessary, be explained to the client. A full explanation of its meaning in the light of present case law is given at 2.7.

An alternative clause might be:

I GIVE AND BEQUEATH absolutely to such of my children as shall be living at the date of my death and if more than one equally between them all my household furniture and effects to be divided as they shall agree between themselves but in default of agreement the decision as to the division of such household furniture and effects shall be made by my trustees as they see fit and their decision shall be absolute and binding upon my said children.

5.9   Pecuniary legacies

A suggested clause might be:

I GIVE the following legacies free of Inheritance Tax

(a) to my brother [name] the sum of one thousand pounds (£1,000);

(b) to my friend [name] the sum of five hundred pounds (£500).

Any tax payable in respect of a pecuniary legacy will be a testamentary expense (see s 34(3) and Sched 1, Pt II of the Administration of Estates Act 1925) in so far as the legacy is payable out of the general personal estate. It is, however, a very long standing practice of will drafters to provide that pecuniary legacies should be 'free of tax'. This is because a pecuniary legacy might become payable out of the proceeds of a sale of a mixed fund of realty and personalty. In this situation, unless a contrary intention was expressed, the legatee would formerly have been liable (*Re Owers* [1941] Ch 17) to bear a proportion of tax on realty, which was for a long time thought not to be a testamentary expense for the purposes of estate duty and capital transfer tax. This position has now been reversed by s 211 of the Inheritance Tax Act 1984. Consequently, unless expressly directed to be liable to tax, no pecuniary legacy is now liable to a charge for tax.

5.10 Charitable gifts

Often, a testator wishes to make gifts to charities and a clause such as the following would suffice:

I GIVE to the [name and address of charity] the sum of £_____ for its general purposes and I declare that the receipt of the person who appears to the Trustees to be the treasurer or other proper officer of that Charity shall be a full and sufficient discharge to my Trustees for such legacy and that my Trustees shall not be concerned to see to the application thereof AND I further DECLARE that if at the date of my death the Charity has ceased to exist or amalgamated with another Charity or has changed its name my Trustees shall pay this legacy to a charitable organisation which they may in their absolute discretion consider most nearly fulfils the objects of the Charity.

Usually it is wise to state the name of the person who, as treasurer of the charity, provides the receipt for the gift.

The effect of this clause is not only to give the legacy to charity, but provides what will happen if the charity ceases to exist. It also provides for a valid receipt of the legacy to be given on behalf of the charity.

5.11 Permission by the terms of will for a beneficiary to reside in real property

Often, a testator will wish to ensure a beneficiary has a continued right to reside in a house/flat. It is best to create an expressed trust for sale with power to postpone sale (note this is not affected by the Trusts of Land and the Trustees Act 1996). A specimen clause as follows would be advisable:

I GIVE my house known as [address] ('the House') which includes any house or flat acquired pursuant to clause (1)(b) below to my Trustees to hold on trust for sale but with power to postpone the sale and in accordance with the following directions:

(1) [full name] ('the Occupant') may live in the House and use it as his/her principal place of residence so long as he/she wishes and without any charge and so long as this paragraph applies:

   (a) the Occupant shall pay all council tax and outgoings and keep the House in good repair and insured to the satisfaction of my Trustees;

   (b) the House shall not be sold without the consent of the Occupant but my Trustees may sell it at the request of the Occupant and buy another residence to which the provisions of this paragraph shall then apply.

(2) On paragraph (1) ceasing to apply the House or any proceeds of sale of the same shall form part of my Residuary Estate.

The clause provides that the beneficiary must pay all outgoings, which could give rise to difficulty. An alternative (if the trustees hold the residue on a continuing trust) would be to give the trustees a discretion as to payment of outgoings and a power to pay them out of the income or capital of the general residue. Note that, although no sale may be made without the beneficiary's consent, the question of the purchase of a substitute residence is left to the discretion of the trustees, so that the beneficiary remains dependent on their decisions.

Now, s 12 of the Trusts of Land and Appointment of Trustees Act 1996 gives a statutory right for a beneficiary with a beneficial interest in position even if he is not of full age to occupy the land subject to a trust of land if the purposes of the trust include making the land available for the occupation by him or the trustees acquire the land in order to make it so available. There is no power to exclude s 12, but a declaration that the purpose of the trust is not for the occupation of land may be made. To do this, it would be advisable to include a specimen clause such as 'the purposes of any trust created by this will do not include making land available for the occupation of any beneficiary although my trustees have the power to do so if they so wish'.

5.12 Gifts of residue

Gifts of the residue or bulk of the estate are very important, otherwise, where there is no gift of residue, the residuary estate will devolve in accordance with the intestacy rules (see 2.7). A standard form clause of residuary gift upon trust for sale and conversion is set out below:

(1) I GIVE DEVISE AND BEQUEATH all my real property and the residue of my personal estate whatsoever and wheresoever situate including any property over which I may have a general power of appointment or disposition except that my property in Spain shall devolve in accordance with the terms of and provisions of my Spanish Will to my Trustees UPON TRUST to sell call in and convert into money the same at such time or times and in such manner as they shall think fit with full power in their absolute discretion to postpone such sale calling in and conversion of the whole or any part or parts of the same during such period as they shall think proper and to retain the same or any part thereof in its actual condition or state of investment without being responsible for loss and I DIRECT that income of so much of the same as shall for the time being remain unsold shall as

well during the first year after my death as afterwards be applied as if the same were income arising from the investments hereafter directed to be made out of the proceeds of sale thereof and no reversionary or other property not actually producing income shall be treated as producing income for the purposes of this my Will.

(2) MY TRUSTEES shall hold the net proceeds of such sale calling in and conversion together with my ready money and any property for the time being remaining unconverted upon the following trusts:

(a) upon trust to pay thereout all my just debts funeral and testamentary expenses and subject thereto.

(b) upon trust absolutely for such of my said sons as shall survive me and in equal shares if more than one PROVIDED THAT if any of them shall die in my lifetime but leaving issue living at my death such issue shall take by substitution and if more than one in equal shares *per stirpes* the share of and in my residuary estate which such deceased son would have taken had he survived me but so that no issue shall take whose parent is living at my death and capable of taking.

Note that *per stirpes* means through each stock of descent.

Trustees, unless expressly exonerated, would be liable for non-conversion of any unauthorised investments within a reasonable time, but the words 'with full power in their absolute discretion to postpone such calling in and conversion during such period as they think proper without being responsible for loss' will authorise the retention of existing unauthorised investments (which, in the absence of this clause, is a contravention of the Trustee Investment Act 1961).

The reader will note that where there is, for example, a Spanish will made by the testator in respect of his Spanish property, it should be made clear that only his English property passes under this will, and therefore, the Spanish property is excepted in the manner and form above.

Note: a trust for sale is created for the reasons referred to in 5.11 and so as to bring into effect the doctrine of conversion.

Before the Trusts of Land and Appointments of Trustees Act, it was usual to impose an expressed trust for sale of residue because otherwise, if the residue included land, the Settled Land Act 1925 would apply and a strict settlement would arise. Since 1 January 1997, no new strict settlements can be created in law. Under the 1996 statute, all trusts which include land are 'trusts of land' and the trustees have wide powers to deal with the land.

Hence, the main reason for creating an expressed trust for sale no longer exists. Trustees have the power to sell or retain land at their discretion. However, it appears there is some doubt about whether trustees who do not hold an expressed trust for sale have the power to sell personality. For this reason (and also for clarity reasons), it may be prudent to impose an express trust for sale. The alternative solution may be to include in the will a power giving the trustees an expressed power to sell personality.

5.13 Gift of residue: life interest

(a) Life interest to spouse

The residue should be given to the trustees on trust for sale with power to postpone sale, with a direction to pay debts, funeral and testamentary expenses and legacies from the proceeds. The trustees are directed to hold the residue on trust and to pay the income to the testator's spouse during her lifetime. The testator should consider whether further flexibility is needed in case the income should prove insufficient for the spouse's needs. The trustees' powers may be extended to allow the trustees to advance or lend capital to the spouse. The testator may wish to separate the matrimonial home from the gift of residue, either by leaving it to the spouse absolutely or by giving the spouse a right of residence.

(b) Remainder to children

The matters to be considered in drafting an immediate gift to children are also relevant in drafting the interests in remainder. Thus, the interests in remainder may be given to the children by name or by description, their interests may be vested or contingent and provision for substitution of grandchildren may be included.

The nature of the children's interests in remainder during the surviving spouse's lifetime should also be considered. Regardless of age, their interests may be made contingent on surviving both parents, with substitutional provisions to take effect where a child dies after the testator but before the surviving spouse, leaving children of his own living at the spouse's death.

(c) Life interest to spouse with remainder to children

I GIVE all the rest of my estate to my Trustees on trust for sale with full power to postpone sale and after payment of my debts funeral and testamentary expenses and legacies to hold the residue ('my Residuary Estate') on the following trusts:

(1) to pay the income to my husband Robert Brown during his lifetime; and then

(2) to pay my Residuary Estate to such of my children Graham Brown, Richard Brown and Catherine Brown as shall be living at the death of the survivor of myself and my husband and if more than one in equal shares provided that if any of my said children shall die before me or before attaining a vested interest leaving children living at the death of the survivor of myself and my husband then such children shall on attaining 18 take by substitution and if more than one in equal shares the share of my Residuary Estate which his her or their parent would have taken if he or she had attained a vested interest.

In this clause, the children are named, probably because there is no question of further children being born. The children's interests do not vest until the death of the surviving spouse so that if a child dies before the life tenant, that child's interest will devolve under the testatrix's will. Alternatively, the children could be given vested interests in remainder, leaving them free to dispose of their interests in their lifetime or by will.

5.14 Accruer clauses

Accruer clauses are aimed at preventing an intestacy applying to a share or shares (normally in the residuary estate) which, for some reason, fail or determine, for example:

If any share or shares in my residuary estate shall fail or determine then from the date of such failure or determination such a share or shares shall accrue and be added to the other share or shares in my residuary estate (equally if more than one) which shall not have failed or determined at the date of my death and be held subject to the same provisions and conditions as those affecting such other share or shares.

5.15 Power of investment and extended powers of maintenance and advancement

The statutory powers of maintenance and advancement in respect of minors under ss 31 and 32 of the Trustee Act 1925 are limited. For a detailed account of trustees' powers, see Parker and Mellows, *The Modern Law of Trusts*, Sweet & Maxwell.

Likewise, the trustees' power of investment is limited by the provisions of the Trustee Investments Act 1961 and the clause which follows effectively extends both the powers of advancement and maintenance, and investment under the respective Acts:

I DECLARE that my Trustees shall have the following powers in addition to their powers under the general law:

(a) I declare that any money liable to be or required to be invested under this my Will may be invested in the purchase of or at interest upon the security of such stocks funds shares securities or other investments of whatsoever nature and wheresoever situate and whether involving liability or not or upon such personal credit with or without security as my Trustees shall in their absolute discretion think fit to the intent that my Trustees shall have the same full and unrestricted powers of investing and transposing investments in all respects as if they were absolutely entitled thereto beneficially. The Trustee Act 2000 gives personal representatives and trustees all the powers to make investments as if they were absolute owners (see Chapter 7).

(b) Without intending to derogate from the statutory powers of maintenance and advancement conferred by ss 31 and 32 of the Trustee Act 1925 I declare that my Trustees may at any time or times in their absolute discretion apply any part or parts of the capital (up to the whole extent) of a share or any part or parts of the capital (up to the whole extent of a share or interest in my residuary estate of a beneficiary hereunder for the maintenance education advancement benefit or advantage of such beneficiary in any such way as my Trustees shall think fit.

(c) Whenever my Trustees shall determine hereunder to apply any income or capital for the maintenance support or benefit of a minor they may either themselves apply that income or capital or pay the same to the parent or guardian of such minor without seeing to the application thereof and without regard to the means of such parent or guardian or to the amount of any other income of such minor.

5.16 Duty to consult beneficiaries

Trustees exercising any function in relation to land must consult any beneficiary who is of full age and beneficially entitled to an interest in possession in land, and so far as consistent with the 'general interests of the trust' give effect to the wishes in any such beneficiary (s 11 of the 1996 Act). The duty to consult may be excluded by a clause in the trust instrument such as 'the provisions of s 11 of the Trusts of Land and the Appointment of Trustees Act 1996 shall not apply so that it shall not be necessary for my trustees to consult any beneficiaries before carrying out any function relating to the land'.

5.17 Control of trustees by beneficiaries

Section 19 of the 1996 Act provide that where the beneficiaries are *sui juris* and together entitled to the whole fund, they may direct the trustees to retire and appoint new trustees of the beneficiaries' choice. Therefore, in a case where the beneficiaries could by agreement end the trust under the rule in *Saunders v Vautier* (1841) 4 Beav 115, they now have the option of allowing the trust to continue with trustees of their choice. The provision may be expressly excluded by the settlor. The drafter should consider the provisions of the trust to discern whether the position might arise where all the beneficiaries are in existence and over 18, but the trust has not ended. If this is possible, then the testator may well wish to prevent the beneficiaries from choosing their own trustees by such a clause as 'the provisions of s 19 of the Trusts of Land and the Appointment of Trustees Act shall not apply to any trust created by this will so that no beneficiary shall have the right to require the appointment or retirement of any trustee or trustees'.

5.18 Power of appropriation

Sometimes, a legatee wishes property forming part of the deceased's estate to be appropriated to him in satisfaction of a pecuniary legacy (for example, taking a clock or other item forming part of the deceased's estate in lieu of the gift of money).

Under s 41 of the Administration of Estates Act 1925, the consent of the persons beneficially entitled to the estate (or certain other persons) is required for such appropriation, and therefore, frequently, a clause is inserted to allow the trustees to appropriate the deceased's assets without obtaining the necessary consents.

Such a clause might read as follows:

I DECLARE that my Trustees may exercise the power of appropriation under s 41 of the Administration of Estates Act 1914 without obtaining any consents required by that section.

Previously, in accordance with the decision in *Jopling v IRC* [1940] 2 KB 282, *ad valorem* stamp duty of 2% was payable on such appropriation, but this liability was abolished by s 84 of the Finance Act 1985 for transfers effected on or after 25 March 1985.

5.19 Carrying on of a business

If the deceased was a sole trader, such as a newsagent, it is essential for the will to contain a clause permitting the executors and trustees to carry on the business so as to preserve its goodwill and allow them to postpone sale of the business until the most appropriate time.

The clause should also cover any personal liability which might be incurred by the executors in the course of carrying on the deceased's business (for a useful explanation of the legal position in these circumstances, refer to Mellows, *The Law of Succession*, Butterworths, p 350).

An appropriate clause might be:

MY TRUSTEES may in their absolute discretion whether or not in their own names or in the name of a company including one incorporated by them for that purpose carry on any trade or business including that of a newsagent or tobacconist which is carried on by me at the date of my death and I declare that in the carrying on of the said trade or business my Trustees shall have the following powers namely:

(a) to retain and employ in the said trade or business or withdraw therefrom the whole or any part of my capital employed in the said business at the date of my death and to use for the general purposes of the said business any additional part of the capital forming part of my said estate which they in their absolute discretion deem expedient;

(b) to employ in the said business such assistants during such period at such remuneration and upon such terms and conditions as they see fit;

(c) to leave the entire management of the said business to any manager or managers whom my trustees may appoint for that purpose at such remuneration and upon such terms and conditions and with such powers and authorities as my trustees may delegate or otherwise agree;

(d) to discontinue the business and wind up the affairs of the said business when and as they see fit;

(e) to sell the said business upon such terms and conditions as they in their absolute discretion determine;

(f) to charge the assets of the said trade or business with the payment of debts incurred in carrying on the same including moneys borrowed from a bank for the purpose of the business together with any liability for interest thereon.

PROVIDED ALWAYS that my said Trustees shall not be responsible to my estate or any beneficiary or person interested therein for any loss incurred by carrying on my said business and I declare that my Trustees shall be jointly and severally indemnified out of my estate against all liability and expenses incurred in connection with the carrying on of my said business.

5.20 Power to insure

The power to insure ought to be given to the trustees in respect of all trust property:

I DECLARE that my Trustees shall have power to insure against loss or damage by fire or from any other risk any property for the time being comprised in my estate to any amount and even though a person may be absolutely entitled to the property and to pay the insurance premium out of the income or capital of my estate or the property itself and any money received by my Trustees under such a policy shall be treated as it if were the proceeds of sale of the property insured.

Under s 19 of the Trustee Act 1925, the power of trustees and personal representatives to insure any building or other property against loss or damage by fire is limited to up to three-quarters of the value of the property. As the trustees will normally wish to insure against all risks and up to the full value of the property, the powers must be extended as in the specimen clause. The power to insure has been extended by the Trustee Act 2000 (see Chapter 7).

5.21 Power to exclude the rules of apportionment of income

The rules as to apportionment of income in respect of trust funds are so complicated and expensive to administer that a wise practitioner will insert a clause excluding them. This will entail specifically excluding the effects of the Apportionment Act 1879 and those rules derived from *Howe v Earl of Dartmouth* (1802) 7 Ves 137; *Allhusen v Whittell* (1867) LR 4 Eq 285 and *Re Earl of Chesterfield's Trust* (1883) 24 Ch D 643, as set out in the precedent clause below. For explanation of the effect of these rules, see Parker and Mellows, *The Modern Law of Trusts*.

> I DECLARE that my Trustees may treat as income all the income from any part of my estate whatsoever the period in respect of which it shall accrue and shall disregard the Apportionment Acts 1834 and 1870 and any Acts replacing them and the rules of equity relating to apportionments including those known as the rules in *Howe v Earl of Dartmouth* and *Allhusen v Whittell* in all their branches.

5.22 Professional charging clause

It is very important for anyone in legal practice to appreciate that since an executor cannot benefit from a trust he administers, if a member of a firm is appointed in person as an executor or trustee of a will, he cannot make a professional charge to obtain probate of the will or do any work as executor or trustee unless a clause is inserted in the will expressly directing that he may charge for all his work, including purely administrative tasks – hence the inclusion of the words 'could have done personally'.

> I DECLARE that any Executor or Trustee hereof being a solicitor or other person engaged in any profession or business or trade shall be entitled to be paid all usual professional business and trade charges for business transacted time expended and acts done by him or any employee or partner of his in connection with the trusts hereof including acts which an Executor or Trustee not being in any profession business or trade could have done personally.

The payment of remuneration to a trustee will no longer be treated as a gift, but as remuneration for services, thereby nullifying the effect of s 15 of the Wills Act 1837, which made any gift to an attesting witness void (see Chapter 7).

5.23 Survivorship clause

A perennial problem for those who draft wills has been the possibility that husbands and wives may die in circumstances where it is impossible to determine who died first.

Therefore, the practice has evolved of incorporating in wills a survivorship clause so that one spouse will only benefit under the other spouse's will if she survives him (or vice versa) by a specified period, commonly 28 days. Section 92 of the Inheritance Tax Act 1984 provides that, where property is held for any person on condition that he survives another for a specified period not exceeding six months, the termination of the other's interest will not give rise to a charge to Inheritance Tax.

The disposition of the property is deemed to have taken effect at the testator's death in favour of the beneficiary who takes on failure of the gift to the other person.

Note that a survivorship clause is often appropriate in wills between spouses if the poorer spouse wishes to avoid assets passing through the estate of the wealthier spouse and thereby suffering higher rates of tax on the latter's death. However, the effect of the spouse exemption should be borne in mind, and also quick succession relief, which makes such clauses of little advantage for fiscal purposes.

Where the beneficiary is not a spouse, the use of the survivorship clause would avoid a double charge to tax; but this may be effected independently by quick succession relief under s 141 of the Inheritance Tax Act 1984. (See 4.3 for full details and rates of quick succession relief currently in force.) The clause might read:

> No person shall take any benefit under this my Will (or any codicil thereto) unless he or she survives me by twenty-eight clear days and any person not so surviving me shall be deemed to have predeceased me and accordingly the income (if any) of every part of my estate shall be treated as accruing after the expiration of twenty-eight days.

Under s 92 of the Inheritance Tax Act 1984, it is now irrelevant whether the second beneficiary is entitled to the intermediate income, thus overruling the position under *Re Jones' Will Trusts; Soames v AG* [1947] Ch 48.

5.24 Receipts by minors

A minor (that is, a person under 18) cannot give a valid receipt for a legacy and therefore a clause to meet this situation is often included.

> MY TRUSTEES may if they in their absolute discretion think fit at any time pay transfer or deliver a legacy under clauses ___ and ___ to the beneficiary though he or she is under age or to his or her parent or guardian on behalf of such beneficiary and the receipt of such beneficiary or of such parent or guardian shall be a complete discharge to my Trustees.

5.25 Statement under the family provision legislation

To counteract family provision claims a statement may be included in the will in the following terms:

I HAVE made no provision by this my Will for my son at his request for reasons known to us and in giving effect to his wishes I record my appreciation of his action and generosity.

5.26 Testimonium and attestation clauses

To give effect to s 9 of the Wills Act 1837, it is advisable to include a standard testimonium and attestation clause despite the relaxation of the rules as to formalities under s 17 of the Administration of Justice Act 1982. Most practitioners use a clause similar to the following:

> Signed by testator the said [name] for [his/her] last Will in the presence of us both being present at the same time who at [his/her] request and in [his/her] presence and in the presence of each other have hereunto subscribed our names as witnesses [witnesses' signatures, addresses and occupations].

According to the provisions of s 9 of the Wills Act 1837 (as amended), a testator must sign or acknowledge his signature in the presence of two witnesses.

The following clause covers the situation where the will is signed by the testator although not in the presence of both witnesses, but where he later acknowledges his signature in their joint presence and before they sign themselves:

> Signed by the testator on the _____ day of _____ 20__
>
> Signature of testator _____
>
> Signed by the testator as and for his last Will and Testament and subsequently acknowledged by him in the presence of us both present at the same time and then signed by us in his presence and in the presence of each other this_____ day of _____ 20__
>
> Signatures, etc of _____
>
> two witnesses _____

Where the testator is blind or illiterate, r 13 of the Non-Contentious Probate Rules 1987 SI 1987/2024 provides that:

> Before admitting to proof a will which appears to have been signed by a blind or illiterate testator or by another person by direction of the testator, or which for any other reason raises doubt as to the testator having had knowledge of the contents of the will at the time of its execution, the registrar shall satisfy himself that the testator had such knowledge.

In these circumstances, the registrar will normally be satisfied if there is evidence that the will has been read over to the testator, and he understood and approved the contents of it. To avoid doubt and in order to satisfy the Probate Registrar in accordance with r 13, the following attestation clause should be incorporated in the will:

Signed by the testator as and for his last Will and Testament

Signature of testator _____

Signed by the testator as his last Will in the presence of us both present at the same time and then signed by us in his presence all the signatures having been added after this said Will had been read over to the testator who is blind [illiterate] by [name person] when the testator seemed thoroughly to understand and approve the contents of the said Will.

Signatures, etc of _____

the two witnesses _____

Note: (1) If the testator placed his mark (that is, an 'X'), rather than his signature, the clause would be slightly altered to read: 'the testator placed his mark on this document being his last Will', and then continue as before.

(2) It is usual practice to request the person who read over the will to the testator to be one of the witnesses.

A will may be signed by some other person in the testator's presence and by his direction (s 9 of the Wills Act 1837 (as amended)). Where this occurs, in order to avoid any problem arising on application for a grant of probate of the will, it is good practice to include an attestation clause in these terms:

Signed by me this _____ day of _____ 20__

Signed by [name and address of signatory] [in his own name on behalf of the testator] in the presence of us both present at the same time and at the direction and in the presence of the testator and then signed by us in the presence of the testator all signatures having been added to this Will after the document had been read over to the testator by [name and address of person who read over the will] at which time the testator seemed thoroughly to understand and approve the contents of the Will.

Signatures, etc of the two witnesses _____

Note: the will can be signed in the signatory's own name or that of the testator – in the latter case substitute the words 'in his own name on behalf of the testator' with the words 'in the name of the testator'.

Clearly, this attestation clause should be adapted to the circumstances, for example, where the testator is incapable of signing only, or incapable of both reading and signing the will.

5.27 Specimen codicil

A specimen codicil might be worded as follows:

> This is a codicil to the last Will and Testament of me [name and address] which Will is dated the _____ day of _____ 20__
>
> 1. I revoke the legacy of £_____ given to _____ by clause [number] of my said Will and in substitution for that legacy I give him the sum of £_____
>
> 2. In all other respects I confirm my said Will.
>
> Signed by the Testator the said _____ as and for a codicil to his last Will and Testament of the _____ day of _____ 20__ [then as attestation clause].

Clause 2 will be sufficient to republish the original will, that is, make it speak as to persons, not at the date of the original will, but rather those in existence at the date of the codicil (see doctrine of republication referred to at 2.6).

5.28 Protection of inheritance

It is sometimes the case that wealthy testators may suspect their sons (or daughters) of having a tendency to waste their inheritance or squander it – if this is the situation, there are two possible remedies:

(a) to defer the vesting of the son's (daughter's) interest in the capital until he/she is aged, say, 30 and give the trustees power to advance the income and capital in the normal way under ss 31 and 32 of the Trustee Act 1925 subject to the rules against excessive accumulation of income; or

(b) to impose a form of discretionary trust, known as a protective trust, which is provided for by s 33 of the Trustee Act 1925.

The first remedy is more commonly used today.

A protective trust has the effect of making the interest of the principal beneficiary (for example, the son or daughter) determinable on bankruptcy, attempted alienation and the like, and thereupon a discretionary trust arises in favour of the principal beneficiary and certain other persons.

For the possibility of a series of protective trusts, see the comment on *Re Richardson's Will Trusts* [1958] Ch 504; (1958) 74 LQR 182.

Such trusts can be created by setting out the trusts expressly, but it is now more common to take advantage of s 33 of the Trustee Act 1925, the effect of which is that certain trusts are implied in any trust coming into operation after 1925 if any income is directed to be held on protective trusts for the benefit of any person ('the principal beneficiary') for the period of his life or any lesser period. In this case, subject to any modification by the trust instrument itself during the above period ('the trust period'), the income is (without prejudice to any prior interest) held:

(a) upon trust for the principal beneficiary until he whether before or after the termination of any prior interest) does or attempts to do or suffers any act or thing, or until any event happens, other than an advance under any statutory or express power, whereby if the ... income were payable during the trust period to the principal beneficiary absolutely during that period, he would be deprived of the right to receive the same or any part thereof; and thereafter,

(b) upon trust for the application thereof for maintenance or benefit of all, or any one or more, of the following persons, namely:

- the principal beneficiary and his or her spouse and issue; or if there is no spouse or issue

- the principal beneficiary and the persons who, if he were dead, would be entitled to the trust property or the income, as the trustees in their absolute discretion think fit.

NB: please refer to the interesting decision of *Hambro v Duke of Marlborough* [1994] Ch 158.

6 Example Precedents

6.1 Will of a married person survived by a spouse and children

THIS IS THE LAST WILL AND TESTAMENT

– of me – David Morcambe

of 6 Sunnyside Avenue, Southport in the

County of Merseyside, banker

1. I HEREBY REVOKE all former Wills and testamentary dispositions made by me and declare this to be my last Will.

2. I APPOINT my wife Julia Morcambe of 6 Sunnyside Avenue, aforesaid and my solicitor Geoffrey Luck of 6 Warren Place Southport (hereinafter called 'my Trustees' which expression shall include the Trustee or Trustees for the time being hereof) to be the Executors and Trustees of this my Will.

3. I APPOINT my mother Miriam Morcambe of 11 Taylor Street, Liverpool in the County of Merseyside, and my mother-in-law Diane Murphy of 2 Winckley Street, Liverpool jointly to be the testamentary guardians of my minor children after the death of my wife.

4. I GIVE DEVISE AND BEQUEATH all my real and personal estate of whatsoever nature and wheresoever situate (including any property over which I may have a general power of appointment or disposition by Will) to my Trustees upon trust to sell call in and convert the same into money with full power in their absolute and uncontrolled discretion to postpone such calling in and conversion for so long a period as they shall think fit without being responsible for loss.

5. MY TRUSTEES shall hold the net proceeds of such sale calling in and conversion together with my ready money and any property for the time being remaining unconverted upon the following trusts:

(a) Upon trust to pay thereout all my just debts funeral and testamentary expenses and subject thereto.

(b) Upon trust absolutely for my wife Julia Morcambe if she shall survive me for the period of twenty-eight clear days but if my said wife shall die in my lifetime or shall not survive me for the period aforesaid or if her interest under the provisions of this clause shall fail for any other reason and subject thereto.

(c) Upon trust absolutely for such of my child or children as shall survive me and attain the age of eighteen years and in equal shares if more than one PROVIDED THAT if any of my said child or children shall die in my lifetime or after my death but under the age of eighteen years leaving a child or children who shall attain the age of eighteen years such child or children shall take by substitution and in equal shares if more than one the share or interest in my residuary estate which such deceased child of mine would have taken had he or she survived me and attained a vested interest under this my Will PROVIDED THAT if the trusts declared by this sub-clause (c) of this my Will shall fail entirely and subject thereto.

(d) Upon trust absolutely for such of my mother and father as shall survive me and in equal shares if both.

6. I DECLARE that my Trustees shall have the following powers in addition to their powers under the general law:

(a) I declare that any money liable to be or required to be invested under this my Will may be invested in the purchase of or at interest upon the security of such stocks funds shares securities or other investments of whatsoever nature and wheresoever situate and whether involving liability or not upon such personal credit with or without security as my Trustees shall in their absolute discretion think fit to the intent that my Trustees shall have the same full and unrestricted powers of investing and transposing investments in all respects as if they were absolutely entitled thereto beneficially.

(b) Without intending to derogate from the statutory powers of maintenance and advancement conferred by ss 31 and 32 of the Trustee Act 1925 I declare that my Trustees may at any time or times in their absolute discretion apply any part or parts of the capital (up to the whole extent) of a share or interest in my residuary estate of a beneficiary hereunder for the maintenance education advancement benefit or advantage in any such way as my Trustees shall think fit of such beneficiary.

(c) Whenever my Trustees shall determine hereunder to apply any income or capital for the maintenance support or benefit of a minor they may either themselves apply that income or capital or pay the same to the parent or guardian of such minor without seeing to the application thereof and without regard to the means of such parent or guardian or to the amount of any other income of such minor.

7. I DECLARE that any Trustees hereof being a Solicitor or an Accountant or other person engaged in any profession or business or trade shall be entitled to be paid all usual professional business and trade charges for business transacted time expended and acts done by him or any employee or partner of his in connection with the trusts thereof including acts which a Trustee not being in any profession business or trade could have done personally.

8. I DECLARE that my Trustees may exercise the power of appropriation conferred by s 41 of the Administration of Estates Act 1925 without obtaining any of the consents required by that section and even though he she or they may be beneficially interested in the property appropriated.

9. I DIRECT that all interest dividends and other payments in the nature of income arising from my estate and received after my death in respect of a period wholly or partly before my death shall be treated as accruing wholly after my death and shall not be apportioned.

10. I DECLARE that all income accruing wholly or partly before the date but received after the date when a beneficiary under my Will shall attain a vested interest in income shall not be apportioned but shall be applied as income received wholly after such attainment of a vested interest.

11. I DECLARE that in any case where my Trustees have an obligation or a discretion under the provisions of my Will or under the general law to pay or apply income or capital to a minor for his or her benefit my Trustees may discharge that obligation or exercise that discretion if they so desire by paying the same to any parent or guardian of the minor and their respective receipts shall be a sufficient discharge to my Trustees who shall not be obliged to see to the application of the income or capital so paid.

12. I DECLARE that my Trustees shall have power to insure against loss or damage by fire or from any other risk any property for the time being comprised in my estate to any amount and even though a person may be absolutely entitled to the property and to pay the insurance premium out of the income or capital of my estate or the property itself and any money received by my Trustees under such

a policy shall be treated as if it were the proceeds of sale of the property insured.

13. I DECLARE that my Trustees may treat as income all the income from any part of my estate whatsoever for the period in respect of which it shall accrue and to disregard the Apportionment Acts 1834 and 1870 and any Acts replacing the rules of equity relating to apportionments including those known as the rules in *Howe v Earl of Dartmouth* and *Allhusen v Whittell* in all their branches.

14. Every person who would otherwise benefit under this my Will but who fails to survive me for twenty-eight clear days shall be treated for all the purposes hereof and for the purposes of the devolution of my estate as having predeceased me and my estate and the intermediate income thereof shall devolve accordingly to the intent that no person shall be entitled to any intermediate income from my estate or any part of it if he dies within that period or acquire therein or in any part thereof a vested interest (or a vested interest subject to defeasance) before the end of it.

15. I DESIRE that my body be cremated and my ashes disposed of by my Trustees and the expense thereof shall be a first charge on my estate.

IN WITNESS whereof I have hereunto set my hand this day of Two thousand and _____

SIGNED by the Testator in

our presence and attested by   _____

us in his presence and in the   _____

presence of each other   _____

6.2   Will of a bachelor or widower survived solely by nephews

THIS IS THE LAST WILL AND TESTAMENT

– of me – Jonathon Jones

of 6 Lot Road, Southport in the County of Merseyside, a clerk

1. I HEREBY REVOKE all former Wills and testamentary dispositions made by me and declare this to be my last Will.

2. I APPOINT my nephews Richard Smith of 17 Dorset Avenue, Southport, Merseyside and Ronald Taylor of 6 Moore Road, Southport, and my solicitor Geoffrey Luck of 6 Warren Place,

Southport aforesaid (hereinafter called 'my Trustees' which expression shall include the Trustee or Trustees for the time being hereof) to be Executors and Trustees of this my Will.

3. I BEQUEATH the following pecuniary legacies free of Inheritance Tax:

   (a) To the Priest in charge for the time being of the Roman Catholic Dioceses of the sum of Four hundred pounds (£400) to provide stipends for the offering of masses for the repose of my soul.

   (b) To the Archbishop for the time being of the Roman Catholic Archdiocese of Liverpool the sum of One thousand pounds (£1,000) to be applied for the purposes of the Priests' Training Fund of the said Archdiocese.

   (c) To my sister-in-law Joanne Smith of 17 Dorset Avenue, aforesaid the sum of Five hundred pounds (£500) and my three Parker-Knoll chairs.

   (d) To my said nephew Richard Smith the sum of One thousand pounds (£1,000).

   (e) To my said nephew Ronald Taylor the sum of One thousand pounds (£1,000).

4. I GIVE DEVISE AND BEQUEATH all my real and the residue of my personal estate of whatsoever nature and wheresoever situate unto my Trustees upon trust to sell call in and convert the same into money with full power in their absolute and uncontrolled discretion to postpone such sale calling in and conversion for so long a period as they shall think fit without being responsible for loss.

5. MY TRUSTEES shall hold the net proceeds of such sale calling in and conversion together with my ready money and any property for the time being remaining unconverted upon the following trusts:

   (a) Upon trust to pay thereout all my just debts funeral and testamentary expenses and subject thereto.

   (b) Upon trust absolutely for such of them my said nephews Richard Smith and Ronald Taylor as shall survive me and in equal shares if more than one PROVIDED THAT if any of them shall die in my lifetime leaving a child or children living at my death such child or children shall take by substitution and in equal shares if more than one the share or interest in my residuary estate which such deceased nephew of mine would have taken had he survived me.

6. I DECLARE that my Trustees shall have the following powers in addition to their powers under the general law:

(a) I declare that any money liable to be or required to be invested under this my Will may be invested in the purchase of or at interest upon the security of such stocks funds shares securities or other investments of whatsoever nature and wheresoever situate and whether involving liability or not or upon such personal credit with or without security as my Trustees shall in their absolute discretion think fit to the intent that my Trustees shall have the same full and unrestricted power of investing and transposing investments in all respects as if they were absolutely entitled thereto beneficially.

(b) Without intending to derogate from the statutory powers of maintenance and advancement conferred by ss 31 and 32 of the Trustee Act 1925 I declare that my Trustees may at any time or times in their absolute discretion apply any part or parts of the capital (up to the whole extent) of a share or interest in my residuary estate of a beneficiary hereunder for the maintenance education advancement benefit or advantage in any such way as my Trustees shall think fit of such beneficiary.

(c) Whenever my Trustees shall determine hereunder to apply any income or capital for the maintenance support or benefit of a minor they may either themselves apply that income or capital or pay the same to the parent or guardian of such minor without seeing to the application thereof and without regard to the means of such parent or guardian or to the amount of any other income of such minor.

7. I DECLARE that in the professed execution of the trusts hereof no Executor or Trustee shall be liable for any loss to my estate by reason of any improper investment made in good faith or for the negligence or fraud of any agent employed by them or by any other Trustee hereof whether or not the employment of such agent was strictly necessary or expedient or by reason of any mistake or omission made in good faith by any Trustee hereof or by reason of any other matter or thing except the wilful and individual fraud or wrongdoing on the part of the Trustee who is sought to be made liable.

8. I DECLARE that any Trustee hereof being a solicitor or other person engaged in any profession or business or trade shall be entitled to be paid all usual professional business and trade charges for business transacted time expended and acts done by him or any employee or partner of his in connection with the trusts hereof including acts which a Trustee not being in any profession business or trade could have done personally.

9. I DECLARE that my Trustees may exercise the power of appropriation conferred by s 41 of the Administration of Estates Act 1925 without obtaining any of the consents required by that section and even though he she or they may be beneficially interested in the property appropriated.

10. I DIRECT that all interest dividends and other payments in the nature of income arising from my estate and received after my death in respect of a period wholly or partly before my death shall be treated as accruing wholly after my death and shall not be apportioned.

11. FOR the purposes of this my Will any children *en ventre* at the date of my death or any other death or event referred to in my Will but born alive in due time thereafter shall be deemed to be living at that date.

12. I DECLARE that if before my death (or after my death but before my Trustees have given effect to the gift in question) any charitable or other body to which a gift is made in this my Will has changed its name or has amalgamated with or transferred all its assets to any other body then my Trustees shall give effect to the gift as if it had been made (in the first case) to the body in its changed name or (in the second case) to the body which results from such amalgamation or to which the transfer has been made.

13. I DECLARE that in any case where my Trustees have an obligation or a discretion under the provisions of my Will or under the general law to pay or apply income or capital to a minor for his or her benefit my Trustees may discharge that obligation or exercise that discretion if they so desire by paying the same to any parent or guardian of the minor and their respective receipts shall be sufficient discharge to my Trustees who shall not be obliged to see the application of the income or capital so paid.

14. I DECLARE that all income accruing wholly or partly before the date but received after the date when a beneficiary under my Will shall attain a vested interest in income shall not be apportioned but shall be applied as income received wholly after such attainment of a vested interest.

15. I DECLARE that if at the time when a legacy is payable to a beneficiary under this my Will he or she shall not have attained the age of eighteen years then the receipt of his or her parent or guardian shall be sufficient discharge to my Trustees.

16. I DECLARE that the receipt of the person who professes to be the Treasurer or other proper office of a charitable body or institution

benefiting under this my Will shall be a full and sufficient discharge to my Trustees.

IN WITNESS whereof I have hereunto set my hand this _____ day of Two thousand and _____

SIGNED by the Testator in

our presence and attested by   _____

us in his presence and in the   _____

presence of each other   _____

6.3 Will of a sole trader giving residue (including his business of newsagent and tobacconist) to trustees with power to carry on the business

THIS IS THE LAST WILL AND TESTAMENT

– of me – Edward Robert Smith

of 22 Kenwood Road, Southport in the County of Merseyside,

Newsagent and Tobacconist

1   I HEREBY REVOKE all former Wills and testamentary dispositions heretofore made by me and declare this to be my last Will.

2.   I APPOINT my solicitor Geoffrey Luck of 6 Warren Place, Southport aforesaid and my accountant John Elsby of 17 King Street, Southport aforesaid (hereinafter called 'my Trustees' which expression shall include the Trustee or Trustees for the time being hereof) to be the Executors and Trustees of this my Will.

3.   I GIVE the following legacies free of Inheritance Tax:

   (a) to my nephew Samuel Smith the sum of one thousand pounds (£1,000);

   (b) to my friend William Rees the sum of five hundred pounds (£500).

4.   I GIVE to my wife Dorothy Joan Smith of 22 Kenwood Road aforesaid absolutely all my personal chattels as defined by s 55(1)(x) of the Administration of Estates Act 1925.

5.   I GIVE DEVISE AND BEQUEATH all my real and the residue of my personal estate of whatsoever nature and wheresoever situate unto my trustees upon trust to sell call and convert the same into

money with full power in their absolute and uncontrolled discretion to postpone such sale calling in and conversion for so long a period as they shall think fit without being responsible for loss.

6. MY TRUSTEES shall hold the net proceeds of such sale calling in and conversion together with my ready money and any property for the time being remaining unconverted upon the following trust:

   (a) Upon trust to pay thereout all my just debts funeral and testamentary expenses and subject thereto.

   (b) Upon trust absolutely for my wife Dorothy Joan Smith if she shall survive me for the period of twenty-eight clear days but if my wife shall die in my lifetime or shall not survive me for the period aforesaid or if her interest under the provisions of this clause shall fail for any other reason and subject thereto.

   (c) Upon trust absolutely for such of them my children Diane Smith and Albert Thomas Smith as shall survive me and attain the age of eighteen years and in equal shares PROVIDED THAT if the trusts declared by this sub-clause (c) shall fail and determine entirely and subject thereto.

   (d) Upon trust absolutely for such of my mother and father as shall survive me and in equal shares if both.

7. I DECLARE that my Trustees shall have the following powers in addition to their powers under the general law:

   (a) I declare that any money liable to be or required to be invested under this my Will may be invested in the purchase or at interest upon the security of such stocks and funds shares securities or other investments of whatsoever nature and wheresoever situate and whether involving liability or not upon such personal credit with or without security as my Trustees shall in their absolute discretion think fit to the intent that my Trustees shall have the same full and unrestricted powers of investing and transposing investments in all respects as if they were absolutely entitled thereto beneficially.

   (b) Without intending to derogate from the statutory powers of maintenance and advancement conferred by ss 31 and 32 of the Trustee Act 1925 I declare that my Trustees may at any time or times in their absolute discretion apply any part or parts of the capital (up to the whole extent) of a share or interest in my residuary estate of a beneficiary hereunder for the maintenance education advancement benefit or advantage in any such way as my Trustees shall think fit of such beneficiary.

(c) Whenever my Trustees shall determine hereunder to apply any income or capital for the maintenance support or benefit of a minor they may either themselves apply that income or capital or pay the same to the parent or guardian of such minor without seeing to the application thereof and without regard to the means of such parent and guardian or to the amount of any other income of such minor.

8.   I DECLARE that any Trustee hereof being a Solicitor or an Accountant or other person engaged in any profession or business or trade shall be entitled to be paid all usual professional business and trade charges for business transacted time expended and acts done by him or any employee or partner of his in connection with the trusts hereof including acts which a Trustee not being in any profession business or trade could have done personally.

9.   I DECLARE that my Trustees may exercise the power of appropriation conferred by s 41 of the Administration of Estates Act 1925 without obtaining any of the consents required by that section and even though he or she or they may be beneficially interested in the property.

10. I DIRECT that all interest dividends and other payments in the nature of income arising from my estate and received after my death in respect of a period wholly or partly before my death shall be treated as accrued wholly after my death and shall not be apportioned.

11. I DECLARE that all income accruing wholly or partly before the date but received after the date when a beneficiary under my Will shall attain a vested interest in income shall not be apportioned but shall be applied as income received wholly after such attainment of a vested interest.

12 I DECLARE that in any case where my Trustees have an obligation or a discretion under the provisions of my Will or under the general law to pay or apply income or capital to a minor for his or her benefit my Trustees may discharge that obligation or exercise that discretion if they so desire by paying the same to any parent or guardian of the minor and their respective receipts shall be sufficient discharge to my Trustees who shall not be obliged to see to the application of the income or capital so paid.

13. I DECLARE that my Trustees shall have power to insure against loss or damage by fire or from any other risk any property for the time being comprised in my estate to any amount and even though a person may be absolutely entitled to the property and to pay the insurance premium out of the income or capital of my estate or the property itself and any money received by my Trustees under such

a policy shall be treated as if it were the proceeds of sale of the property insured.

14. I DECLARE that my Trustees may treat as income all the income from any part of my estate whatsoever the period in respect of which it shall accrue and to disregard the Apportionment Acts 1834 and 1870 and any Act replacing them and the rules of equity existing to apportionments including those known as the rules in *Howe v Dartmouth* and *Allhusen v Whittell* in all their branches.

15. EVERY person who would otherwise benefit under this my Will but who fails to survive me for twenty-eight clear days shall be treated for all the purposes hereof and for the purposes of the devolution of my estate as having predeceased me and my estate and the intermediate income thereof shall devolve accordingly to the intent that no person shall be entitled to any intermediate income from my estate or any part of it if he dies within that period or acquire therein or in any part thereof a vested interest (or a vested interest subject to defeasance) before the end of it.

16. MY TRUSTEES may in their absolute discretion whether or not in their own names or in the name of a company including one incorporated by them for that purpose carry on any trade or business including that of a newsagent or tobacconist which is carried on by me at the date of my death and I declare that in the carrying on of the said trade or business my Trustees shall have the following powers namely:

   (a) to retain and employ in the said trade or business or withdraw therefrom the whole or any part of my capital employed in the said business at the date of my death and to use for the general purposes of the said business any additional part of the capital forming part of my said estate which they in their absolute discretion deem expedient;

   (b) to employ in the said business such assistants during such period at such remuneration and upon such terms and conditions as they see fit;

   (c) to leave the entire management of the said business to any manager or managers whom my trustees may appoint for that purpose at such remuneration and upon such terms and conditions and with such powers and authorities as my trustees may delegate or otherwise agree;

   (d) to discontinue the business and wind up the affairs of the said business as they see fit;

(e) to sell the said business upon such terms and conditions as they in their absolute discretion determine;

(f) to charge the assets of the said trade or business with the payment of debts incurred in carrying on the same including moneys borrowed from a bank for the purpose of the business together with any liability for interest thereon.

PROVIDED ALWAYS that my said Trustees shall not be responsible to my estate or any beneficiary or person interested therein for any loss incurred by carrying on my said business and I declare that my Trustees shall be jointly and severally indemnified out of my estate against all liability and expenses incurred in connection with the carrying on of my said business.

17. The statutory power of appointing new trustees of this my Will shall be exercised by my wife during her widowhood.

IN WITNESS whereof I have hereunto set my hand this _____ day of Two thousand and _____

SIGNED by the Testator in

our presence and attested by   _____

us in his presence and in the   _____

presence of each other   _____

6.4   Nil band legacy will

THIS is the last will

– of me – Edward Robert Smith

of 22 Kenwood Road, Southport in the County of Merseyside

which I make this Twenty-fifth day of June Two thousand and ___

1. I HEREBY REVOKE all former Wills and testamentary dispositions made by me and declare this to be my last Will.

2   I APPOINT my solicitor Geoffrey Luck of 6 Warren Place, Southport, Merseyside and my Accountant John Elsby of 17 King Street, Southport, Merseyside to be the Executors and Trustees of this my Will and I DECLARE that the expression my Trustees wherever used in this my Will shall mean unless the context otherwise requires the Trustees or Trustee for the time being hereof whether original or substituted.

3. (A) IF MY said wife Dorothy Joan Smith shall survive me by the period of one calendar month (but not otherwise) I GIVE to my Trustees such a sum as shall be equal to the upper limit of the nil per cent band (at the time of my death) in the Table in Sched 1 to the Inheritance Tax Act 1984 (or any statutory modification or re-enactment thereof) less an amount equal to the aggregate of:

   (a) the value for the purpose of Inheritance Tax of any chargeable transfers of value made by me in my lifetime and which fall to be cumulated with the value of my estate on my death for Inheritance Tax purposes; and

   (b) all bequests contained in any codicil hereto which are not exempt transfers of value for the purposes of Inheritance Tax;

   (c) all other property (if any) which is treated as property to which I am beneficially entitled immediately before my death (including property subject to a reservation as defined by s 102 of the Finance Act 1986) and which is chargeable to Inheritance Tax by reason of my death;

   (d) all or any settled property in which on my death I have an interest in possession (as that expression has meaning for the purposes of the Inheritance Tax Act 1984) and which is chargeable to Inheritance Tax by reason of my death.

   (B) MY TRUSTEES shall hold the sum given to them by paragraph (A) of this clause on the trusts and with and subject to the powers and provisions hereinafter declared.

   (C) IN THIS clause the following expressions have the following meanings respectively:

   (a) 'the Discretionary Legacy' means the sum referred to in paragraph (A) of this clause and the investments and property for the time being representing the same;

   (b) 'the Trust Period' means the period of eighty years from the date of my death;

   (c) 'the Accumulation Period' means the period of twenty-one years from the date of my death;

   (d) 'the Discretionary Objects' means:

      (i) my said wife;

      (ii) my children and my remoter issue (whether living at my death or born thereafter);

      (iii) the respective spouses, widows and widowers of my said children and remoter issue.

(D)

(a) MY TRUSTEES shall hold the capital and income of the Discretionary Legacy upon trust for all or such one or more exclusively of the other or others of the Discretionary Objects at such age or time or respective ages or times and if more than one in such shares and either absolutely or for such period or respective periods and with such gifts over and with or subject to such discretionary trusts powers or provisions (whether at the discretion of my Trustees or of any of them or of any one or more of the Discretionary Objects or of any other person or persons) and generally in such manner in all respects for the benefit of all or any one or more of the Discretionary Objects as my Trustees (being at least two in number or a trust corporation and without infringing the rules against perpetuities and against excessive accumulations) may at any time or times or from time to time during the Trust Period by deed revocable or irrevocable appoint.

(b) IN DEFAULT of and until and subject to any appointment made under the last foregoing sub-paragraph my Trustees shall hold the capital and income of the Discretionary Legacy upon the following trusts and with and subject to the following powers that is to say:

(i) my Trustees shall have power during the Accumulation Period to pay or apply all or so much (if any) of the income of the Discretionary Legacy as my trustees shall from time to time in their discretion think fit to or for the benefit of all or such one or more exclusively of the other or others of the Discretionary Objects for the time being in existence and if more than one in such proportions and in such manner in all respects as my Trustees shall from time to time in their discretion think fit;

(ii) subject thereto my Trustees shall during the Accumulation Period accumulate the income of the Discretionary Legacy in the way of compound interest by investing the same and the resulting income thereof from time to time in any manner hereinafter authorised as an accretion to the capital of the Discretionary Legacy and as one fund with such capital for all purposes;

(iii) subject thereto my Trustees shall during the Trust Period pay or apply the income of the Discretionary Legacy to or for the benefit of all or such one or more exclusively of the other or others of the Discretionary Objects for the time being in existence and if more than one in such proportions and in such manner in all respects as my Trustees shall from time to time in their discretion think fit;

(iv) subject thereto my Trustee shall hold the capital and income of the Discretionary Legacy upon trust for such of my children and remoter issue as shall be living immediately before the expiration of the Trust Period if more than one in equal shares *per stirpes* and not *per capita* absolutely.

(E) I DECLARE that any appointment or determination under any of the foregoing provisions of this clause by the persons who shall constitute my Trustees shall be given effect notwithstanding that at any time such appointment or payment is made Probate of this my Will may not have been granted or that the administration of my estate may not have been completed.

4. I GIVE all my property of whatsoever nature and wheresoever situate not hereby or by a codicil hereto otherwise effectually disposed of (including any property over which I have a general power of appointment or disposition by Will) unto my Trustees upon trust that my Trustees shall sell call in and convert into money the same at such time or times and in such manner as they shall think fit with power to postpone such sale calling in and conversion of the whole or any part or parts of the same during such period as they think proper and to retain the same or any part thereof in its actual condition or state of investment without being responsible for loss and I direct that the income of so much of the same as shall for the time being remain unsold shall as well during the first year after my death as afterwards be applied as if the same were income arising from investments hereinafter directed to be made out of the proceeds of sale thereof and that no reversionary or other property not actually producing income shall be treated as producing income for the purposes of this my Will.

5. (A) MY TRUSTEES shall out of the moneys to arise from the sale calling in and conversion of or forming part of my said property pay my funeral and testamentary expenses (including all duties and taxes hereinafter directed to be borne by my residuary estate) and my debts and the legacies given by this my Will or by any codicil hereto and the rule of equity known as the rule in *Allhusen v Whittell* shall be disregarded.

(B) I DECLARE that subject as herein elsewhere provided all Inheritance Tax and other duties and taxes (if any) payable on or by reason of my death (including any such duties and taxes as may be payable outside the United Kingdom) in respect of my estate shall be borne by my residuary estate and the expression 'free of tax' in this my Will or any codicil hereto shall mean free of Inheritance Tax and such duties and taxes as aforesaid.

6. MY TRUSTEES shall invest the residue of the said moneys at such time or times as they shall think fit in or upon any of the investments hereinafter authorised with power to vary or transpose such investments for or into others of a nature hereby authorised and shall hold such investments and so much of the said residue as shall for the time being remain uninvested and so much of my said property as shall for the time being remain unsold and the property from time to time representing the same respectively (all of which premises are hereinafter called 'the Trust Fund') upon the trusts hereinafter declared concerning the same.

7. MY TRUSTEES shall hold the capital and income of the Trust Fund upon the following trusts:

    (A) in trust for my said wife absolutely if she shall survive me by the period of one calendar month and so that during such period the income of the Trust Fund shall be accumulated and shall only be paid to my said wife if she survives me by the said period of one calendar month;

    (B) if my said wife shall not survive me by the period of one calendar month or the gift under the terms of this my Will shall fail for any reason my Trustees shall hold the Trust Fund (and any accumulations of income thereof) in trust for such of my children living at my death and if more than one in equal shares PROVIDED ALWAYS that if any child of mine shall have predeceased me leaving a child or children him or her surviving who attain the age of twenty-one years such child or children of my deceased child shall take and if more than one in equal shares the share of the Trust Fund which his/her or their parent would have taken had he or she survived me.

8. FOR THE avoidance of doubt I DECLARE that unless the context otherwise requires the provisions of clauses 9 to 26 inclusive shall apply to the Discretionary Legacy referred to in clause 3 hereof as well as to the Trust Fund.

9. SECTION 31 of the Trustee Act 1925 (as amended by s 1 of the Family Law Reform Act 1969) shall apply in relation to the trusts of this my Will as if there had been omitted so much of the proviso to sub-section (1) of the said s 31 as enacts that where trustees have notice that the income of more than one fund is applicable for the purposes therein mentioned a proportionate part only of the income of each fund shall be paid or applied for those purposes.

10. SECTION 32 of the Trustee Act 1925 shall apply in relation to the trusts of this my Will as if paragraph (a) of the proviso to sub-section (1) thereof had been omitted and as if the words 'advancement education or benefit' had been substituted for the words 'advancement or benefit' PROVIDED that no payment or application of capital money thereunder may be made unless the person thereby advanced educated or benefited will either at once or on or before attaining the age of twenty-five years become entitled to or to an interest in possession in the whole amount so paid or applied.

11. ALL MONEYS liable to be invested under the trusts of this my Will may be applied or invested in the purchase or other acquisition of any property of whatsoever nature and wheresoever situate and whether or not subject to incumbrances or involving liability of any kind (including the purchase or improvement of a freehold or leasehold dwelling house anywhere in the world for use as a residence and the acquisition effecting or maintaining of a policy or policies of assurance or insurance and the lending or deposit of money with or without any personal or other security and upon any terms and conditions whatsoever) to the intent that my Trustees shall have the same full free and unrestricted powers of investment and of changing investments as if they were absolutely entitled to such moneys beneficially.

12. MY TRUSTEES shall not be bound (in exercising the powers conferred on them by the last foregoing clause or otherwise) to have regard to any statutory or other requirement as to diversification of investments belonging to a trust nor shall any beneficiary hereunder be entitled to compel the sale or other realisation of any property not producing income or the investment of any part of the Trust Fund in property producing income.

13. MY TRUSTEES may at any time or times in their discretion revocably delegate to any person or persons (whether or not being one or more of my Trustees and whether or not carrying on business in the management of investments) for the time being considered suitable by my Trustees all or any of my Trustees' powers and discretions as to the investment of the Trust Fund or any part thereof and the management retention or realisation of any security or other property comprised therein upon such terms as to remuneration and otherwise and in such manner generally as my Trustees in their discretion may from time to time think fit and my Trustees may make or authorise payment out of the capital or income of the Trust Fund of the remuneration of any such person or persons.

14. ANY LAND that may in any circumstances become vested in my Trustees (except any land situate elsewhere than in England or Wales

to which my Trustees in their discretion may determine that this proviso shall be inapplicable) shall be held by my Trustees upon trust for sale with full power to postpone such sale.

15. THE BENEFIT of the occupation use or enjoyment of any land or chattels subject to the trusts hereof may in the discretion of my Trustees and subject to such terms and conditions in all respects as my Trustees may think fit be treated as income of the Trust Fund and my Trustees may at any time or times in their discretion lay out any money then subject to the trusts hereof in the purchase or other acquisition of any land or chattels for the purpose of enabling the same to be occupied used or enjoyed accordingly.

16. ANY PROPERTY subject to the trusts hereof may at any time in the discretion of my Trustees be vested in any person or persons (whether or not being one or more of my Trustees) in any part of the world as nominee or nominees for my Trustees.

17. MY TRUSTEES shall have power in their discretion from time to time to open and operate any banking account or accounts in their name with such bank or banks in any part of the world as they may think fit and may pay any moneys forming part of the Trust Fund or the income thereof to the credit of any such account and (without being responsible for loss) may deposit with any such bank for safe custody any securities certificates documents of title or other papers or documents or valuables comprised in or relating to the Trust Fund or any part thereof and may from time to time give to any bank such directions as to the custody or release of any such items as they may think fit, and my Trustees may at any time or times delegate revocably to any two or more of their number or to a single corporate trustee all or any of their powers under the foregoing provisions of this clause.

18. MY TRUSTEES may at any time or times in their discretion lend any money then subject to the trusts hereof either with or without any personal or other security to any beneficiary for the time being hereunder or to the executors administrators or trustees of any estate or trust in which such beneficiary is beneficially interested or make any property subject to the trusts hereof available as security for any loan raised or to be raised by any such beneficiary or by any such executors administrators or trustees in each case subject to such terms and conditions in all respects as my Trustees may think fit to impose and notwithstanding that the borrower or one or more of the borrowers may be a trustee or trustees hereof.

19. MY TRUSTEES may at any time or times in their discretion borrow or raise by mortgage or charge of any property subject to the trusts

hereof such money as they may think fit and treat such money in like manner in all respects as if it were money forming part of the Trust Fund.

20. MY TRUSTEES shall in respect of any property subject to the trusts hereof have all the powers of management and exploitation of an absolute beneficial owner (including in particular and without prejudice to the generality of the foregoing expressions all the powers of leasing accepting surrenders of leases building improvement repair and insurance of such an owner) and may in the exercise of such powers make any outlay of income or capital.

21. MY TRUSTEES both after and during the administration of my estate may exercise the powers as to appropriation conferred on personal representatives by s 41 of the Administration of Estates Act 1925 without any of the consents made requisite by that section and I DECLARE that within the period of two years after my death my Trustees shall be entitled to exercise the power conferred by this clause by valuing the property to be allotted appropriated partitioned or apportioned either as at the date of my death or as at the date of such allotment appropriation partition or apportionment as they shall in their absolute discretion think fit and any such allotment appropriation partition or apportionment shall be final and binding on all beneficiaries interested in my estate and none of my trustees shall be liable for or the consequences of any such allotment appropriation partition or apportionment.

22. I DECLARE that all dividends rents interest or money in the nature of income which shall actually be paid after my death or other event which otherwise would or might require to be apportioned shall be deemed to have been received by my Trustees in respect of a period wholly subsequent to my death or other event as the case may be and so that no apportionment thereof shall be made.

23. I DECLARE that any of my Trustees may join in exercising any discretion or power notwithstanding that he or she may have a personal interest in whether such discretion or power is exercised or in whether such discretion or power is exercised in any particular way.

24. I DECLARE that my Trustees shall have power to insure against loss or damage by fire or from any other risk any property for the time being comprised in my estate to any amount and even though a person may be absolutely entitled to the property and to pay the insurance premium out of the income or capital of my estate or the property itself and any money received by my Trustees under such

a policy shall be treated as if it were the proceeds of sale of the property insured.

25. ANY OF my Trustees being a solicitor accountant or other individual engaged in any profession or business shall be entitled to be paid all usual professional or other charges and retain all usual commissions for work or business done or transacted by or through him or his firm in connection with the trusts hereof whether in the ordinary course of his profession or business or not and although not of a nature requiring the employment of such professional or business person.

26. ANY POWER (including this power) by this my Will conferred on my Trustees may in their discretion be by deed extinguished or restricted or wholly or partially released notwithstanding that the same is of a fiduciary nature.

IN WITNESS whereof I have to this my Will contained on this and the preceding _____ sheets of paper set my hand the day and year first before written

SIGNED by the said

Edward Robert Smith as and for his

_____

last Will in the presence of us both

_____

present at the same time who at his

_____

request in his presence and in the   _____

presence of each other have hereunto

_____

subscribed our names as witnesses

_____

NB: if the benefit of the nil band rate legacy of this form is to be used, it is essential that both spouses make wills whereby one of the discretionary objects in the case of the husband is his wife and the case of the wife is her husband.

6.5   Memorandum of wishes

It is generally a good idea when preparing nil band discretionary wills also to draw up a letter of wishes for the spouses. These letters of wishes are not legally binding, but merely an expression by the testator as to his wishes.

TO THE EXECUTORS AND TRUSTEES OF MY WILL

dated the _____ day of _____ 20__

By Clause 3 of my Will I have left a legacy on discretionary trusts for the benefit of my family.

The purpose of this memorandum is to record my wishes as to how I would like you to exercise the discretionary powers conferred on you.

First, I would like you to regard my wife as the primary beneficiary and would expect you to pay the whole of the income to her during her lifetime. In addition, you should make payments out of capital to her to meet any reasonable request she may make. Payments of income or capital should only be made to other beneficiaries if requested by my wife.

After my wife's death I would expect the trust to be wound up and distributed equally to my children (or the children of any deceased child) at an age when you consider they are able to handle an inheritance.

I appreciate that my wishes are not legally binding and that in any event circumstances may arise which may make my wishes inappropriate. However, subject to unforeseen and special circumstances, I hope you will be able to act in accordance with my views.

Dated this _____ day of _____ 20__

Signed _____

(Testator/testatrix's signature)

6.6 Living will precedent of the Voluntary Euthanasia Society

LIVING WILL

TO MY FAMILY, DOCTOR AND ALL OTHER PERSONS CONCERNED

THIS DIRECTIVE is made by me (full name in capitals) _____

_____

of (address) _____

at a time when I am of sound mind and after careful consideration.

I DECLARE that if at any time the following circumstances exist, namely:

1 I suffer from one or more of the conditions mentioned in the schedule; and

2 I have become unable to participate effectively in decisions about my medical care; and

3 Two independent doctors (one a consultant) are of the opinion that I am unlikely to recover from illness or impairment involving severe distress or incapacity for rational existence,

THEN AND IN THOSE CIRCUMSTANCES my directions are as follows:

1 that I am not to be subjected to any medical intervention or treatment aimed at prolonging or sustaining life;

2 that any distressing symptoms (including any caused by lack of food or fluid) are to be fully controlled by an appropriate analgesic or other treatment, even though that treatment may shorten life.

I consent to anything proposed to be done or omitted in compliance with the directions expressed above and absolve my medical attendants from any civil liability arising out of such acts or omissions.

I wish it to be understood that I fear degeneration and indignity far more than I fear death. I wish my medical attendants and any person consulted by them to bear this statement in mind when considering what my intentions would be in any uncertain situation.

I RESERVE the right to revoke this DIRECTIVE at any time, but unless I do so it should be taken to represent my continuing directions.

SCHEDULE

A Advanced disseminated malignant disease (for example, widespread lung cancer).

B Severe immune deficiency (for example, AIDS).

C Advanced degenerative disease of the nervous system (for example, motor neurone disease).

D Severe and lasting brain damage due to injury, stroke, disease or other cause.

E Senile or pre-senile dementia (for example, Alzheimer's disease).

F Any other condition of comparable gravity.

*I nominate (name in capitals) _____

of (address) _____

(telephone number) _____

as a person to be consulted by my medical attendants when considering what my intentions would be in any uncertain situation.

*Delete if not applicable

My General Practitioner is (name of GP) _____

of (address) _____

(telephone number) _____

*Before signing this directive I have talked it over with my GP.

*Delete if not applicable

Signed _____

Date _____

WE TESTIFY that the maker of this directive signed it in our presence, and made it clear to us that he/she understood what it meant. We do not know of any pressure being brought on him/her to make such a directive and we believe it was made by his/her own wish. So far as we are aware, we do not stand to gain from his/her death.

Witnessed by:

Signature: _____ Signature: _____

Name: _____ Name: _____

Address: _____ Address: _____

_____ _____

_____ _____

This directive was reviewed and confirmed by me on the following dates (sign your name each time you enter a date).

Comment

The Voluntary Euthanasia Society in the package compiled not only includes the above draft precedent, but also makes the following statement concerning the precedents legal status. It states:

Although there is no law that governs the use of living wills, in common law refusing treatment beforehand will have a legal effect as long as it meets the following preconditions mainly:

1   The person is mentally able, is not suffering any mental distress and is over 18 when he/she makes the request.

2   The person was fully informed about the nature and consequences of the living will at the time he/she made it.

3   The person is clear that the living will should apply to all situations or circumstances which arise later.

4   The person is not pressurised or influenced by anyone else when he/she made the decision.

5   The living will has not been changed either verbally or in writing since it was drawn up.

6   The person is now mentally incapable of making any decision because they are unconscious or otherwise unfit.

These provisions have been approved in a number of recent legal cases. The Appeal Court, in the case of *Re T* [1992] 4 All ER 649 established that if an informed and capable patient has made a choice which is clearly established and applicable in the circumstances, doctors would be bound by it. This view was confirmed by the later cases of *Airedale NHS Trust v Bland* [1993] 2 WLR 316, HL and *Re C* [1994] 1 All ER 819, which stated that a document was legally binding if it represented an informed refusal of specific treatments. The patient cannot refuse measures which are clearly appropriate in the circumstances and which are provided for all patients. These measures could include basic hygiene such as washing, pain relief and the offer of being fed. Also, the patient cannot refuse treatment where his or her refusal would conflict with existing legal requirements or his or her condition would pose a risk to other patients and medical staff.

6.7   The living will and health care proxy of the Terrence Higgins Trust

Living will advance directives

1   Medical treatment in general

Three possible health conditions are described below. For each condition, choose 'A' or 'B' by ticking the appropriate box, or leave both boxes blank if you have no preference. The choice between 'A' or 'B' is exactly the same in each case. Treat each case separately. You do not have to make the same choice for each one.

I declare that my wishes concerning medical treatment are as follows.

Case 1 Life-threatening condition

Here are my wishes if:

* I have a physical illness from which there is no likelihood of recovery; and

* The illness is so serious that my life is nearing its end.

A   I want to be kept alive for as long as reasonably possible using whatever forms of medical treatment are available.

B   I do not want to be kept alive by medical treatment. I want medical treatment to be limited to keeping me comfortable and free from pain. I refuse all other medical treatment.

Case 2 Permanent mental impairment

Here are my wishes if:

* my mental functions have become permanently impaired;

* the impairment is so severe that I do not understand what is happening to me;

* there is no likelihood of improvement; and

* my physical condition then becomes so bad that I would need medical treatment to keep me alive.

A   I want to be kept alive for as long as reasonably possible using whatever forms of medical treatment are available.

B   I do not want to be kept alive by medical treatment. I want medical treatment to be limited to keeping me comfortable and free from pain. I refuse all other medical treatment.

Case 3 Permanent unconsciousness

Here are my wishes if:

* I become permanently unconscious and there is no likelihood I will regain consciousness.

A I want to be kept alive for as long as reasonably possible using whatever forms of medical treatment are available.

B I do not want to be kept alive by medical treatment. I want medical treatment to be limited to keeping me comfortable and free from pain. I refuse all other medical treatment.

2   Particular treatment or tests

If you have any wishes about particular medical treatments or tests, you can record them here. If you want to refuse a particular treatment or test, you should say so clearly. This is where to write your views about having treatment or tests while you are pregnant. You should speak to your doctor before you write anything in this space.

3   Having a friend or relative with you if your life is in danger

You can fill in this section if you would like a particular person to be with you if your life is in danger. It may not be possible to contact the person you name, or for him or her to arrive in time.

If my life is in danger, I want the following person to be contacted to give him or her a chance to be with me before I die.

Name:

Address:

Daytime phone number: Evening phone number:

Tick this box if you fill in this section, and want to be kept alive for as long as is reasonable to give the person you name a chance to reach you.

If you tick this box, any wishes you have stated above in Section 1 – Medical treatment in general and Section 2 – Particular treatments or tests, may be temporarily disregarded. This is explained in the notes with this form.

LIVING WILL Health care proxy

I appoint the following person to take part in decisions about my medical care on my behalf and to represent my views about the decisions if I am unable to do so. I want him or her to be consulted about and involved in those decisions and I want anyone who is caring for me to respect the views he or she expresses on my behalf.

Name:

Address:

Daytime phone number: Evening phone number:

Signatures

This Living Will remains effective until I make clear that my wishes have changed.

Sign and date the form here in the presence of a witness.

Your signature: Date: / /

The witness must sign here after you have signed the form.

The witness should the print his or her name and address in the spaces provided.

Please read notes to this form to see who should not be a witness.

Signature of witness:

Name of witness:

Address of witness:

LIVING WILL declaration

Your details

I am making this Living Will to record my wishes in case I become unable to communicate, and cannot take part in decisions about my medical care.

Name:

Address:

Daytime phone number: Evening phone number:

If you discuss this Living Will with a doctor before or after you fill it in please fill in this section.

I have discussed this Living Will with the following doctor.

Doctor's name:

Doctor's address:

Doctor's phone number:

Comment

The Terrence Higgins Trust works in conjunction with the Centre of Medical Law and Ethics, King's College London, Strand, WC2R 2LS. The trust is a registered charity providing practical support, help, counselling, advice for anyone living with or concerned about AIDS or HIV infection.

The centre at King's College London is concerned with research and teaching in all aspects of medical law, medical ethics and related public policy issues.

The legal status of a health care proxy is uncertain, but hopefully, doctors will heed what a person's proxy states.

The BMA has issued *Advanced Statement about Medical Treatment – Code of Practice* (report of the BMA, April 1995). It has in addition issued *Advanced Statements – BMA Views* (last revised May 1995) to give guidance to health professionals and doctors about the implementation of advance statements (living wills) by patients in respect of patients' future treatment.

The latter document (*inter alia*) provides guidance on a range of statements, including those specifying treatment preferences, accounts of fundamental life values, advance authorisation of treatment and anticipatory refusals.

7 The Trustee Act 2000

7.1 Introduction

In this chapter, the implications of the Trustee Delegation Act 1999, which came into force earlier this year, and the Trustee Act, which received the Royal Assent on 23 November 2000 and became law by 1 February 2001, are analysed.

The Trustee Delegation Act 1999 is discussed in more detail in the *Law Society Gazette* ((1999) 28 July, p 31). As is obvious from its name, the statute is concerned with the delegation of the powers of trustees.

There are, of course, existing provisions in this respect, namely s 23(1) and (2) of the Trustee Act 1925, which remain unchanged by the new legislation.

Section 25 of the Trustee Act 1925 and s 3(3) of the Enduring Powers of Attorney Act 1985 are subject to substantial amendments by the 1999 enactment.

The changes are referred to in the article in the *Law Society Gazette*, which should be carefully scrutinised along with the article in the Probate Section Journal (October 1999, issue 12, p 8) by Ann Whitfield of McFalanes solicitors.

The Trustee Delegation Act has little direct effect on the law of wills and it is not intended to deal with it in any more detail here.

7.2 The provisions of the Trustee Act

The Trustee Act, which became law on 1 February 2001, makes major changes to the powers of trustees and personal representatives (s 35). It consists of 43 sections and 4 Schedules.

The five main issues which the Act addresses are:

• the duty of care;

- the power of investment;
- the acquisition of land by trustees/personal representatives;
- the power to use agents, nominees and custodians;
- payment for work as a trustee.

Section 1 of the Act is concerned with 'the duty of care'. This is defined by the section as a duty to 'exercise such care and skill as is reasonable in the circumstances'. Regard must be had to: (a) any special knowledge or expertise that the personal representative has or holds himself out as having; and (b) if he acts as a trustee in the course of a business or profession, to any special knowledge or experience that it is reasonable to expect of a person acting in the course of that kind of business or profession.

Schedule 1 states that the duty of care applies, for example, to where the personal representative exercises a general power of investment, carries out some duty in relation to some investments, to his land, appoints any kind of agent, nominee or custodian or exercises a power, for example, to compound a liability or to insure.

The duty of care may be excluded in so far as it appears from the will or trust instrument that the duty is not meant to apply (see Sched 1, para 1).

The power of investment is in s 3 of the Act. The section states that a personal representative or trustee may make any kind of investment that he could make if he were absolutely entitled to the assets of the trust/estate. The general power of investment does not permit a trustee/personal representative to make investments in land other than in loans secured on land.

In exercising the powers of investment, whenever arising, the trustee must have regard to the standard investment criteria (s 4). Under this new power, there is no formal investment restriction so long as the trustees comply with the standard investment criteria.

The 'standard investment criteria' in relation to a will or trust are – s 4(3)(a), the suitability to the trust of investments of the same kind as any particular investment proposed or made or retained and of that particular investment as an investment of that kind and, (b) the need for diversification of investments of the trust in so far as it is appropriate to the circumstances of the trust/estate.

The power of investment may be excluded by the trust instrument but, subject to any such exclusion, is an addition to the powers conferred on the trustees. It shall apply to trusts/wills whenever created.

Buying land: s 8 empowers trustees to acquire freehold or leasehold land in the UK as an investment for the occupation of a beneficiary or for any other reason. A trustee/personal representative who acquires land under this section is to have all the powers of an absolute owner in relation to land (s 8(3)).

Use of agents, nominees and custodians (ss 11–20): s 11 now allows trustees (other than charitable trustees) to delegate certain specific powers.

Trustees may, under s 14, authorise a person to exercise functions as their agent on such terms as to remuneration and any other matter as they see fit.

Generally, trustees may not appoint an agent on any terms which allow for a substitute: (a) to do the work; (b) restrict the liability of the agent to the trustees; (c) give rise to a conflict of interests (s 14(3)).

Trustees will be able to appoint nominees and custodians and, if they wish to invest in bearer securities, they must appoint such a person (s 18).

The appointment must be either in writing or so evidenced and certain conditions must be satisfied, for example, the terms of the appointment should exclude the possibility of substitutes, restricted liability and conflict of interest (s 20(3)).

An appointment of an agent or a nominee is by no means for life.

Under ss 21(1), (2) and (3), trustees should monitor the performance of their agents, nominees and custodians to ensure the terms of the appropriate policy statement and revision to it are complied with.

Where necessary, the trustees must intervene to give the agent new directions or, if necessary, revoke the appointment (s 22(4)).

A 'policy statement' is a statement that gives guidance as to how the agents should exercise their functions (s 15(2a)).

Any agreement under which an agent is to act shall include a term to the effect that the agent will ensure compliance with the policy statement or if the policy statement is revised or replaced under s 22, the revised or replacement policy statement.

Unless the will or trust instrument provides to the contrary (s 29(5)), s 28 provides that a trustee may be paid for services which a layperson may be able to provide.

A new rule which will assist the execution of wills (s 28(4)) entitles the payment of remuneration to a personal representative/trustee to be regarded as remuneration for services not as a gift within s 15 of the Wills Act 1837, which makes void any gift to an attesting witness.

Professional trustees may receive 'reasonable provision' for work done (ss 29(1) and (3)).

Section 19 of the Trustee Act 1925 is repealed by s 34 of the Act, which substitutes a completely new s 19 for the repealed section. Trustees are, by s 34, given the same power to insure property as beneficial owners. It applies to all trustees and extends to the full value of the trust property. The earlier 1925 statute permitted insurance up to three-quarters of the value of the property and refers to loss or damage by fire only. Both the new and old sections provide for payment of the insurance premiums out of the income and capital of the trust fund.

It would seem likely, however, that wills draftsmen will continue to include an express clause (see para 5.20 for a precedent of an express clause as to insurance).

The Act will modernise the powers of personal representatives and trustees so that they accord more meaningfully with modern day practices, and particularly in relation to homemade wills, older trusts and intestate estates.

The importance of the Act is that it extends substantially the powers of personal representatives and might potentially reduce the number of clauses presently inserted in wills.

However, the writer is of the opinion that the Act must be carefully scrutinised and where any doubt arises, express provisions should still be made in the will, for example, in relation to personal representatives, powers of investment and buying.

It should be noted that after the Trustee Act became law, there will be technically no need to extend the powers of insurance by an express clause in the will in the form referred to in specimen clause 5.20, nor is it probably necessary to extend the power of investment as referred to in specimen clause 5.15.

The need for an expressed professional charging clause is no longer technically a necessity in the form set out in specimen clause 5.22.

8 Answers to Common Questions

8.1 Formalities of a will

- **What steps ought a solicitor take in respect of the formal execution of the will?**

Since *Esterhuizen v Allied Dunbar plc* (1998) *The Times*, 10 June, the solicitor has a heavy burden of duty to see the will is formally executed if he is to avoid a claim for negligence. Normally, he should be present when the will is executed rather than post the will to the testator.

- **What steps should be taken where the testator is aged or has suffered a serious illness?**

In the light of *Re Simpson* (1977) 121 Sol Jo 224, it might be advisable to write to the testator's doctor to confirm his capacity to make a will or preferably request a doctor to be present when the will is executed – great caution is necessary in broaching this matter to clients. See 2.3.

- **What steps should be taken if the testator is blind or illiterate?**

The will should contain a special attestation clause to the effect that the will has been read over to the illiterate or blind testator and stating that he understands and approves the contents. See 2.3.

- **What steps ought to be taken where the will is signed not by the testator himself, but by someone else in his presence and by direction?**

A special attestation clause explaining that the will has been signed on behalf of the testator in his presence and by his direction should be incorporated in the will. (For a suggested specimen attestation clause to meet this situation, see Chapter 5). For more detail, see 2.4.

- **What should be done in the rare situation where the testator suffers from insane delusions?**

The written evidence of a medical practitioner must be obtained to confirm that the delusions would not affect the type of dispositions the testator is making. It would be advisable for the written evidence to be placed with the will, and the doctor requested to act as one of the witnesses to the will.

- **If there is a real risk that the testator may become incapable of managing his own affairs for any reason (for example, senility) before his death, what steps should be taken?**

Advise the relatives of the deceased to consider requesting the person in question to sign an enduring power of attorney form so that his affairs can be managed on his behalf in his lifetime. See 2.12.

8.2   Safe keeping of the will

- **What special advice should be given to the testator concerning the safe keeping of the will?**

The testator should be counselled to tell his relatives and/or his executors where his will can be found and his exact funeral wishes, for example, as to cremation, burial or use of parts of the body for transplant. If the testator prefers, a note can be prepared to be placed with his possessions in a place where his relatives might be expected to look immediately after his death.

The testator should also be informed of the procedure for deposit of wills with the Principal Probate Registry to save expense and trouble after his death in attempts to trace evidence or otherwise of his will. See 4.7.

8.3 Contemplation of marriage

• **If the testator is contemplating marriage to a particular person, what advice should be given?**

He should be advised to incorporate in the will a clause that his will is in contemplation of marriage to a particular person so as to avoid the rule that his will is revoked by his subsequent marriage and his wishes therefore defeated. See 5.3.

8.4 Tax advice

• **Where the testator has a substantial estate, is there any particular advice he should be given?**

He should be advised as to ways of reducing or mitigating Inheritance Tax by making use of such exemptions as the £250 small gift rule, £3,000 annual expenditure allowance, gifts on marriage and the rules as to potentially exempt transfers if the testator survives seven years after the date of the gift.

Consideration should also be given to Inheritance Tax planning such as, *inter alia*, use of the spouse exemption, equalisation of spouses' estates and the nil band discretionary trust. For a fuller discussion, see 4.3.

8.5 Burial wishes

• **If he has special wishes as to cremation or burial, what should a testator do?**

He should inform his relatives and executors of these wishes at the time of making the will, as the will may not be read until it is too late to give effect to them. See 1.2.

- **If the testator wishes to donate parts of his body, for example, his kidneys, to medical science, are there special steps he should take?**

Yes, he should be advised to carry a donor card on his person stating what parts of his body he would wish to be available for medical and transplant purposes. See 1.2.

An appropriate clause intimating the testator's wishes as to cremation or burial, or donation of parts of his body for therapeutic purposes, should be incorporated in the will.

8.6   Family provision on death

- **Where the testator does not wish a potential claimant to benefit under his will, should he take any special steps?**

He should incorporate in his will, or alternatively leave a statement with his will, oral or in writing, explaining why he has made no provision in his will for the person in question and thereby take advantage of the provisions of s 21 of the Inheritance (Provision for Family and Dependants) Act 1975. See 2.8.

8.7   Clauses in the will

- **Should the testator be given any special advice as to the form of provision he makes in his will?**

He should be advised that residuary gifts are payable after all pecuniary legacies have been satisfied and thus not to make too many pecuniary legacies if his intention is for the bulk of his estate to benefit any particular relative or friend. See 4.4.

- **Should the testator always include substitution clauses in the event of the death of the residuary beneficiary(ies)?**

The testator should always be advised to include substitution clauses in his will in case the beneficiary(ies) of the residuary estate predecease him and an intestacy thereby arises.

- **Where the testator makes a specific gift of property, should he be given any particular advice?**

Yes, he should be advised that, by s 35 of the Administration of Estates Act 1925, where property (for example, the matrimonial home) is subject to, for example, a building society mortgage, he must make it clear whether he wishes the mortgage to be discharged out of the property given to the specific legatee or out of the general residuary estate. See 4.5.

- **Should the testator incorporate any special provision in his will where, at his death, he was a sole trader?**

A sole trader should incorporate in his will a clause permitting the executors/trustees to carry on the business so as to prevent a reduction in value of the goodwill of the business. Power should be given to them to sell the business at the most opportune moment in order to obtain the best price possible for the business. It is also sensible to give the executors/trustees powers as to the employment of money in the business. See 5.19.

- **What steps ought a wealthy testator to take if he fears his children or relatives will squander his estate?**

Incorporate in the will a clause delaying vesting of an absolute interest in them until they attain a specified age (for example, 30 years old) by which age it may be hoped they will have mended their ways; or, as a last resort, incorporate protective trusts under s 33 of the Trustee Act 1925. See 5.28.

8.8   Consideration of a will

- **Where the testator is young and likely to live for some time after making his will, should he be given any particular advice?**

Yes, to consider revising his will and provisions in it in the light of any change in his personal or financial circumstances as the years pass by, particularly if there is a reduction in the size of the estate he will have to leave on death. It is advisable also, on reviewing a will, to clarify the present addresses of all beneficiaries to prevent possible problems of tracing them on death.

- **If he has an occupational pension under his employment, should he be given any special advice?**

Yes, to make sure he designates who is entitled to any death benefit under the scheme and be prepared to change the beneficiaries, particularly if his wife or any of his other dependants should die in his lifetime.

8.9   Children

- **If the testator has any illegitimate children, should he take any special steps to ensure they benefit/do not benefit under the terms of his will?**

It is good practice for a testator to state whether he wishes illegitimate children to take under his will – they are regarded as on an equal footing to his legitimate children in wills executed on or after 1 January 1970 (s 15 of the Family Law Reform Act 1969, as repealed and re-enacted by ss 1 and 19 of the Family Law Reform Act 1987).

- **Should the testator take any special steps to ensure that adopted children will be entitled to benefit under his will?**

No special provision is required in respect of an adopted child (see s 1 of the Adoption Act 1976).

Are stepchildren included in a gift to children or issue?

They are not normally included and, if it is desired to benefit stepchildren, the testator should state so.

8.10 Errors in the will

• **What steps should be taken if there are any errors, even of a purely typographical nature, in the will?**

To prevent the expense of any possible need for an affidavit of plight and condition before probate of the will is granted, it is essential that all alterations, obliterations or interlineations are authenticated by the signature or initials of the testator and witnesses in the margin (see r 14 of the Non-Contentious Probate Rules 1987 SI 1987/2024).

8.11 Revocation

• **Should the testator be given any advice should he wish to revoke the will at a later date?**

He must be informed that destruction by such means as writing 'revoked' across the will will not revoke it, that actual destruction by tearing or burning is essential, or alternatively a new will or codicil with an express revocation clause with intent to revoke should be drawn up. See 2.5.

8.12 General

• **Can a will be incorporated in a deed?**

No, a will cannot be incorporated in a deed, which is, of its very nature, irrevocable, since all wills are ambulatory, that is, capable of dealing with property after the date the will was made, and must be capable of revocation right up to the date of actual death (see *Vynior's Case* (1609) 8 Co Rep 816).

- ## Can a will include a clause to prevent lapse of a gift where the beneficiary predeceases the testator?

No, a clause of this nature is invalid in law (*Re Ladd, Henderson v Porter* [1932] 2 Ch 219) and a substitution clause providing for the property to pass to another beneficiary in the case of lapse must be incorporated.

- ## Does a will attract stamp duty or require production to the Inland Revenue after execution in a similar way to a conveyance or lease?

No stamp duty is payable in respect of a will and the Inland Revenue is not concerned to see it at all.

- ## Why should you always keep a completed draft or photocopy of a client's will?

Because, by the Non-contentious Probate Rules 1987 r 54, on application to the registrar he may admit to probate such draft or copy will, provided an affidavit (that is, sworn evidence) is adduced (r 54(3)) to prove:

(a) the will's existence after the testator's death;

(b) the contents of the will;

(c) where a reconstruction takes place, the accuracy of that reconstruction – a reliable witness can sometimes even prove by oral evidence alone that a will was made and give details of its contents (see *Sugden v St Leonards* (1876) IPD 154 and *Re Yelland* (1975) 119 Sol Jo 562).

- ## Why is it of the utmost importance to date a will?

It is essential to date a will. Where the date is missing or incomplete, or there are conflicting dates, by r 14(4) of the Non-Contentious Probate Rules 1987, the registrar may require 'such evidence as he thinks necessary to establish the date' – probably an affidavit as to due execution of the will.

- ## What do you do if the testator is known by other names or nicknames?

Refer to the testator by his correct name in full with his other name or nickname(s) in brackets with a phrase after the correct names such as 'otherwise known as'.

8.13 Executors/trustees

- ## How important is it to advise on the choice of executors and trustees?

It is very important, since it is essential to appoint businesslike trustees to safeguard the financial interests of beneficiaries (for example, see to valuation of antiques, etc) and also, if there are minor children, to act as quasi-parents and give moral guidance and comfort.

- ## Should substitute trustees/executors always be appointed?

If the original executor or trustee dies, and he is the sole executor and no substitute executors have been appointed, additional expense may be incurred by the need to apply for letters of administration with will annexed instead of an application for a grant of probate. The alternative is to appoint a firm or trust corporation. See 5.5.

8.14 Incidence of debts

- ## Should the liability to pay debts and funeral expenses be expressed in the will?

It is advisable to do so where there is an intention to vary the statutory order laid down in s 34(3) and Sched 1, Pt II of the Administration of Estates Act 1925.

8.15 Gifts to animals, etc

• **What advice should be given to a testator who wishes to leave a gift of money to his pets?**

He should be advised that this will create what is known as a trust of imperfect obligation, that is, that only persons can compel the trustees to carry out the terms of the trust (*The Modern Law of Trusts*, Sweet & Maxwell). Such trusts, although *prima facie* valid, cannot be enforced by the non-human beneficiary and can only be carried out if the trustees agree to do so. The testator should therefore make sure that the trustees he appoints by the terms of his will are prepared to carry out the trust and ensure the gift (usually of money) is used for the benefit of the named animal(s).

8.16 Gifts to charities

• **Should any special steps be taken where the testator leaves property to a charity?**

It is good practice to inform the charity of the gift and ask them whether they wish the gift to be made in any particular form – many charities have special forms of wording relating to gifts made to them.

8.17 Codicils

• **What reaction should a legal adviser have if the testator seeks to make a codicil?**

He should advise the testator that it is preferable to make a fresh will including any amendments rather than make a codicil, because there is always the risk of losing codicils if they become detached from the original will.

9 Useful Addresses

Principal Registry Probate Department
Somerset House
Strand
London WC2R 1LP
020 7936 6948/6974 practitioner's application
020 7936 6983/7459 personal application

District Probate Registries

Registry	Sub-registry
Birmingham	Stoke-on-Trent
The Priory Courts	Combined Court Centre
33 Bull Street	Bethesda Street
Birmingham B4 6DU	Hanley Stoke-on-Trent ST1 3BP
0121 681 3400/3414	Staffs
Fax 0121 681 3404	01782 213736
DX 701990 Birmingham (7)	Fax 01782 201944
	DX 20736 Hanley
Brighton	Maidstone
William Street	The Law Courts
Brighton BN2 2LG	Barker Road
East Sussex	Maidstone ME16 8EQ
01273 684071	Kent
Fax 01273 688281	01622 202048
DX 98073 Brighton (3)	DX 51972 Maidstone (2)

Registry	Sub-registry
Bristol The Crescent Centre Temple Back Bristol BS1 6EP Avon 0117 9273915 Fax 0117 9259377 DX 94400 Bristol (5)	Bodmin Market Street Bodmin PL31 2JW Cornwall 01208 72279 DX 81858 Bodmin
	Exeter Finance House Barnfield Road Exeter EX1 1QX Devon 01392 74515 DX 8380 Exeter
Cardiff Probate Registry of Wales PO Box 474 2 Park Street Cardiff CF1 1ET 029 20376479 DX 122782 Cardiff (13)	Bangor 1st Floor Bron Castell High Street Bangor LL57 1YS Gwynedd 01248 362410 DX 23186 Bangor (2)
	Carmarthen 14 King Street Carmarthen SA31 1BL Dyfed 01267 236238 DX 51420
Ipswich Level 3, Haven House 17 Lower Brook Street Ipswich IP4 1DN Suffolk 01473 253724 Fax 01473 280889 DX 3279 Ipswich	Norwich Combined Court Building The Law Courts Bishopgate Norwich NR3 1UR Norfolk 01603 761776 DX 97385 Norwich (5)

Registry	Sub-registry
Leeds	Peterborough
3rd Floor	1st Floor, Crown Buildings
Coronet House	Rivergate
Queen Street	Peterborough PE1 1EJ
Leeds LS1 2BA	01733 62802
W Yorkshire	DX 12327 Peterborough (1)
0113 2431505	
Fax 0113 2448145	Lincoln
DX 26451 Leeds (Park Square)	Mill House
	Brayford Side North
	Lincoln LN1 1YW
	01522 523648
	DX 11048 Lincoln (1)
Liverpool	Sheffield
Queen Elizabeth II Law Courts	PO Box 832
Derby Square	The Law Courts
Liverpool L2 1XA	50 West Bar
Merseyside	Sheffield S3 8YR
0151 236 8264	S Yorkshire
Fax 0151 236 5575	0114 281 2596
DX 14246 Liverpool (1)	DX 26054 Sheffield (2)
	Chester
	5th Floor
	Hamilton House
	Hamilton Place
	Chester CH1 2DA
	Cheshire
	01244 345082
	DX 22162 Northgate
Manchester	Lancaster
9th Floor	Mitre House
Astley House	Church Street
23 Quay Street	Lancaster LA1 1HE
Manchester M3 4AT	Lancashire
0161 834 4319	01524 36625
Fax 0161 834 5651	DX 63509 Lancaster
DX 14387 Manchester (1)	

Registry

Sub-registry

Newcastle upon Tyne
2nd Floor
Plummer House
Croft Street
Newcastle upon Tyne NE1 6NP
0191 261 8383
Fax 0191 233 0868
DX 61081 Newcastle upon Tyne

Nottingham
Buttdyke House
33 Park Row
Nottingham NG1 6GR
0115 9414288
Fax 0115 9243374
DX 10055 Nottingham

Carlisle
Courts of Justice
Earls Street
Carlisle CA1 1DJ
Cumbria
01228 21751
DX 63034

Oxford
10a New Road
Oxford OX1 1LY
01865 241163
Fax 01865 204402
DX 4337 Oxford (1)

Middlesbrough
Combined Court Centre
Russell Street
Middlesbrough TS1 2AE
Cleveland
01642 340001

York
Duncombe Place
York YO1 2EA
N Yorkshire
01904 671564
DX 61543 York

Winchester
4th Floor
Cromwell House
Andover Road
Winchester SO23 7EW
Hants
01962 853046/863771
Fax 01962 877371
DX 96900 Winchester (2)

Gloucester
2nd floor
Combined Court Building
Kimbrose Way
Gloucester GL1 2DG
01452 522585
DX 7537 Gloucester (1)

Sub-registry

Leicester
5th Floor
Leicester House
Lee Circle
Leicester LE1 3RE
0116 2538558
Fax 0116 2627796
DX 13655 Leicester (4)

Others

Capital Taxes Office
Ferrers House
PO Box 38
Castle Meadow Road
Nottingham NG2 1BB
0115 974 0000/2400
Fax 0115 974 2432

Public Trust Office
(inc Court of Protection)

Stewart House
24 Kingsway
London WC2B 6JX
020 7269 7300 (PTO)
Fax 020 7404 1725

The Terrence Higgins Trust
c/o The Centre of Medical Law and Ethics
Kings College London
Strand
London WC2R 2LS
020 7242 1010

The Voluntary Euthanasia Society
13 Prince of Wales Terrace
London W8 5PG
020 7937 7770

10 Further Reading

10.1 Books

Aldridge, T, *Powers of Attorney*, 9th edn, 1999, London: Sweet & Maxwell

Barlow, J, King, L and King, A, *Administration and Taxation – A Practical Guide*, 7th edn, 1997, London: Sweet & Maxwell

Cretney, S, *Enduring Powers of Attorney*, 3rd edn, 1991, Bristol: Jordans

D'Costa, R, *Holloway's Probate Handbook: Practice and Procedure*, 9th edn, 1993, London: Sweet & Maxwell

Heywood and Massey, *Court of Protection Practice*, 12th edn, 1991, London: Sweet & Maxwell

Kerridge, R, *Parry and Clark's The Law of Succession*, 10th edn, 1995, London: Sweet & Maxwell

Lyons, TJ, *Chapman's Inheritance Tax*, 8th edn, 1989, London: Sweet & Maxwell

Margrave-Jones, C, *Mellows' The Law of Succession*, 5th edn, 1993, London: Butterworths

McKie, S, *Tolley's Estate Planning*, 2000, Croydon: Tolley

Oakley, AJ, *Parker and Mellows' The Modern Law of Trusts*, 7th edn, 1994, London: Sweet & Maxwell

Ray, R, *Ray's Practical Inheritance Tax Planning*, 4th edn, 1999, London: Butterworths

Ross Martin, J, *Theobald on the Law of Wills*, 16th edn, 2000, London: Sweet & Maxwell

Sunnucks, JHG, *Williams, Mortimer and Sunnucks on Executors, Administrators and Probate*, 18th edn, 2000, London: Sweet & Maxwell

White, P, *Post-Death Rearrangements*, 4th edn, 1992, London: Sweet & Maxwell

Whitehouse, C, *Revenue Law – Principles and Practice*, 18th edn, 2000, London: Butterworths

Yeldham, REF *et al*, *Tristram and Coote's Probate Practice*, 27th edn, 1989, London: Butterworths

10.2 Looseleaf works

Bark-Jones, R (gen ed), *Butterworths Wills, Probate and Administration Service*, 1996, London: Butterworths

Millet, P (Sir) (ed), *Encyclopaedia of Forms and Precedents*, London: Butterworths

Withers, *Practical Will Precedents*, continually updated, London: Longman

Potter, DC and Monroe, HH, *Potter and Monroe's Tax Planning with Precedents*, 11th edn, 1988, London: Sweet & Maxwell

Dymond's Capital Taxes, London: Longman

NB: all these looseleaf volumes are updated annually.